·: *The Yale Shakespeare* : ·

THE FIRST PART OF
KING HENRY THE SIXTH

EDITED BY

TUCKER BROOKE

WILDSIDE PRESS

TABLE OF CONTENTS

THE map on the next page is a modified reproduction of one included in the famous Atlas of ORTELIUS (edition of 1580), those places only being indicated which are of interest in connection with the 'First Part of Henry VI' and 'Henry V.' Parallels of latitude are reckoned eastwardly around the globe from a line in the Atlantic Ocean about 20 degrees west of Greenwich; parallels of longitude are as in modern maps. The two lines of dashes mark the approximate limits of English dominion in France prior to the relief of Orleans in 1429. Only the central district, south of the Loire and east of Bordeaux, and the besieged city of Orleans then recognized the Dauphin's authority.

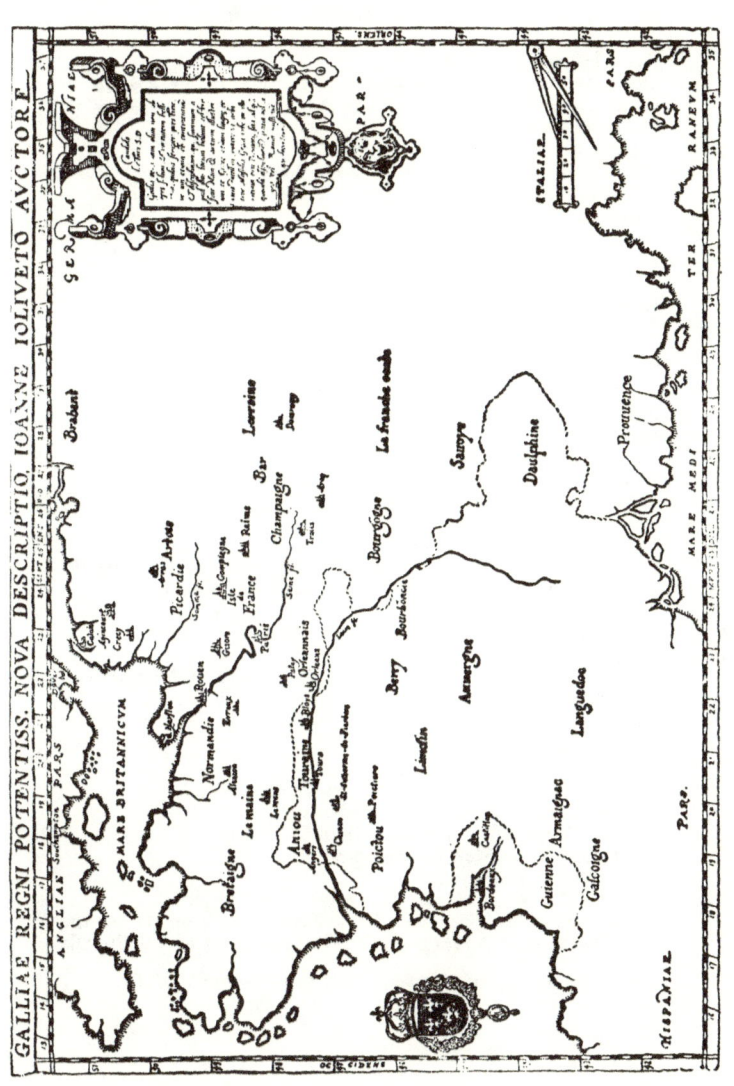

[DRAMATIS PERSONÆ

KING HENRY THE SIXTH
DUKE OF BEDFORD, *Uncle to the King, Regent of France*
DUKE OF GLOUCESTER, *Uncle to the King, and Protector*
DUKE OF EXETER,
BISHOP OF WINCHESTER, } *Great-Uncles to the King*
RICHARD PLANTAGENET, *Son of Richard, late Earl of Cambridge; afterwards Duke of York*
DUKE OF SOMERSET
EARL OF WARWICK
EARL OF SALISBURY
EARL OF SUFFOLK
LORD TALBOT, *afterwards Earl of Shrewsbury*
JOHN TALBOT, *his Son*
EDMUND MORTIMER, *Earl of March*
SIR JOHN FASTOLFE
SIR WILLIAM GLANSDALE
SIR THOMAS GARGRAVE
SIR WILLIAM LUCY
VERNON, *of the White-Rose, or York, Faction*
BASSET, *of the Red-Rose, or Lancaster, Faction*
WOODVILE, *Lieutenant of the Tower*
Mayor of London
A Lawyer of the Temple
Lords, Warders of the Tower, Mortimer's Keepers, Heralds, Officers, Soldiers, Messengers, and Attendants

CHARLES, *Dauphin of France (legitimately, King Charles VII)*
REIGNIER, *Duke of Anjou, and titular King of Naples*
DUKE OF BURGUNDY
DUKE OF ALENÇON
BASTARD OF ORLEANS
Governor of Paris
General of the French Forces in Bordeaux
Master-Gunner of Orleans, and his Son
An old Shepherd, Father to Joan la Pucelle
MARGARET, *Daughter to Reignier*
COUNTESS OF AUVERGNE
JOAN LA PUCELLE, *commonly called Joan of Arc*
French Herald, Sergeant, and Sentinels; Porter to the Countess of Auvergne; Fiends appearing to La Pucelle

SCENE: *London and Westminster; various parts of France.*]

The First Part of Henry the Sixth

ACT FIRST

Scene One

[Westminster Abbey]

Dead March.

Enter the Funeral of King Henry the Fifth, attended on by the Duke of Bedford, Regent of France; the Duke of Gloucester, Protector; the Duke of Exeter; Warwick; the Bishop of Winchester; and the Duke of Somerset [with Heralds, &c.].

Bed. Hung be the heavens with black, yield day to
    night!
Comets, importing change of times and states,
Brandish your crystal tresses in the sky,
And with them scourge the bad revolting stars,
That have consented unto Henry's death!   5
King Henry the Fifth, too famous to live long!
England ne'er lost a king of so much worth.
    Glo. England ne'er had a king until his time.
Virtue he had, deserving to command: 9
His brandish'd sword did blind men with his beams;
His arms spread wider than a dragon's wings;
His sparkling eyes, replete with wrathful fire,   12
More dazzled and drove back his enemies
Than mid-day sun fierce bent against their faces.
What should I say? his deeds exceed all speech:

The First Part, etc.; *cf. n.*   1 Hung . . . black; *cf. n.*
10 his: *iis*

He ne'er lift up his hand but conquered.   16
   Exe. We mourn in black: why mourn we not in
     blood?
Henry is dead and never shall revive.
Upon a wooden coffin we attend,
And death's dishonourable victory   20
We with our stately presence glorify,
Like captives bound to a triumphant car.
What! shall we curse the planets of mishap
That plotted thus our glory's overthrow?   24
Or shall we think the subtle-witted French
Conjurers and sorcerers, that, afraid of him,
By magic verses have contriv'd his end?
   Win. He was a king bless'd of the King of
     kings.   28
Unto the French the dreadful judgment-day
So dreadful will not be as was his sight.
The battles of the Lord of hosts he fought:
The church's prayers made him so prosperous.   32
   Glo. The church! where is it? Had not churchmen
     pray'd,
His thread of life had not so soon decay'd:
None do you like but an effeminate prince,
Whom like a school-boy you may over-awe.   36
   Win. Gloucester, whate'er we like thou art pro-
     tector,
And lookest to command the prince and realm.
Thy wife is proud; she holdeth thee in awe,
More than God or religious churchmen may.   40
   Glo. Name not religion, for thou lov'st the flesh,
And ne'er throughout the year to church thou go'st,
Except it be to pray against thy foes.

16 lift: *lifted*

Bed. Cease, cease these jars and rest your minds
　　in peace!　　　　　　　　　　　　44
Let's to the altar: heralds, wait on us:
Instead of gold we'll offer up our arms,
Since arms avail not, now that Henry's dead.
Posterity, await for wretched years,　　　48
When at their mothers' moist eyes babes shall suck,
Our isle be made a marish of salt tears,
And none but women left to wail the dead.
Henry the Fifth! thy ghost I invocate:　　52
Prosper this realm, keep it from civil broils!
Combat with adverse planets in the heavens!
A far more glorious star thy soul will make,
Than Julius Cæsar, or bright—　　　　56

Enter a Messenger.

Mess. My honourable lords, health to you all!
Sad tidings bring I to you out of France,
Of loss, of slaughter, and discomfiture:
Guyenne, Champagne, Rheims, Orleans,　　60
Paris, Gisors, Poitiers, are all quite lost.
　Bed. What sayst thou, man, before dead Henry's
　　corse?
Speak softly; or the loss of those great towns
Will make him burst his lead and rise from death.　64
　Glo. Is Paris lost? is Roan yielded up?
If Henry were recall'd to life again
These news would cause him once more yield the
　　ghost.
　Exe. How were they lost? what treachery was
　　us'd?　　　　　　　　　　　　68
　Mess. No treachery; but want of men and money.
Among the soldiers this is muttered,

50 marish: *marsh; cf. n.*　　　　60, 61 *Cf. n.*
64 lead: *leaden wrappings*　　　65 Roan: *Rouen*

That here you maintain several factions;
And, whilst a field should be dispatch'd and
    fought,   72
You are disputing of your generals.
One would have lingering wars with little cost;
Another would fly swift, but wanteth wings;
A third thinks, without expense at all,   76
By guileful fair words peace may be obtain'd.
Awake, awake, English nobility!
Let not sloth dim your honours new-begot:
Cropp'd are the flower-de-luces in your arms;   80
Of England's coat one half is cut away.

    Exe. Were our tears wanting to this funeral
These tidings would call forth their flowing tides.

    Bed. Me they concern; Regent I am of France.   84
Give me my steeled coat: I'll fight for France.
Away with these disgraceful wailing robes!
Wounds will I lend the French instead of eyes,
To weep their intermissive miseries.   88

Enter to them another Messenger.

    Sec. Mess. Lords, view these letters, full of bad
    mischance.
France is revolted from the English quite,
Except some petty towns of no import:
The Dauphin Charles is crowned king in Rheims;   92
The Bastard of Orleans with him is join'd;
Reignier, Duke of Anjou, doth take his part;
The Duke of Alençon flieth to his side.   *Exit.*

    Exe. The Dauphin crowned king! all fly to
    him!   96

71 several: *separate*
72 field . . . dispatch'd: *battle . . . arranged*
80 *The fleurs de lys are plucked from your coat of arms*
88 intermissive: *temporarily interrupted (but now to be renewed)*
92 *Cf. n.*

O! whither shall we fly from this reproach?
  Glo. We will not fly, but to our enemies' throats.
Bedford, if thou be slack, I'll fight it out.
    Bed. Gloucester, why doubt'st thou of my forward-
      ness?   100
An army have I muster'd in my thoughts,
Wherewith already France is overrun.

Enter another Messenger.

    Third Mess. My gracious lords, to add to your
      laments,
Wherewith you now bedew King Henry's hearse,
I must inform you of a dismal fight   105
Betwixt the stout Lord Talbot and the French.
    Win. What! wherein Talbot overcame? is 't so?
    Third Mess. O, no! wherein Lord Talbot was o'er-
      thrown: 108
The circumstance I'll tell you more at large.
The tenth of August last this dreadful lord,
Retiring from the siege of Orleans,
Having full scarce six thousand in his troop,   112
By three-and-twenty thousand of the French
Was round encompassed and set upon.
No leisure had he to enrank his men;
He wanted pikes to set before his archers;   116
Instead whereof sharp stakes pluck'd out of hedges
They pitched in the ground confusedly,
To keep the horsemen off from breaking in.
More than three hours the fight continued;   120
Where valiant Talbot above human thought
Enacted wonders with his sword and lance.
Hundreds he sent to hell, and none durst stand him:

110, 111 *Cf. n.*   110 dreadful: *redoubtable*
112 full scarce: *scarce full, not quite*   116 wanted pikes; *cf. n.*

Here, there, and everywhere, enrag'd he flew: 124
The French exclaim'd the devil was in arms;
All the whole army stood agaz'd on him.
His soldiers, spying his undaunted spirit,
A Talbot! A Talbot! cried out amain,   128
And rush'd into the bowels of the battle.
Here had the conquest fully been seal'd up,
If Sir John Fastolfe had not play'd the coward.
He, being in the vaward,—plac'd behind,   132
With purpose to relieve and follow them,—
Cowardly fled, not having struck one stroke.
Hence grew the general wrack and massacre;
Enclosed were they with their enemies.   136
A base Walloon, to win the Dauphin's grace,
Thrust Talbot with a spear into the back;
Whom all France, with their chief assembled strength,
Durst not presume to look once in the face.   140
     Bed. Is Talbot slain? then I will slay myself,
For living idly here in pomp and ease
Whilst such a worthy leader, wanting aid,
Unto his dastard foemen is betray'd.   144
     Third Mess. O no! he lives; but is took prisoner,
And Lord Scales with him, and Lord Hungerford:
Most of the rest slaughter'd or took likewise.
     Bed. His ransom there is none but I shall pay: 148
I'll hale the Dauphin headlong from his throne;
His crown shall be the ransom of my friend;
Four of their lords I'll change for one of ours.
Farewell, my masters; to my task will I;   152
Bonfires in France forthwith I am to make,
To keep our great Saint George's feast withal:

124 flew; *cf. n.*   126 agaz'd on: *astounded at*
131 Sir John Fastolfe; *cf. n.*   132 vaward,—plac'd behind; *cf. n.*
136 with: *by*   148 *Cf. n.*
154 Saint George's feast; *cf. n.*   withal: *therewith*

Ten thousand soldiers with me I will take,
Whose bloody deeds shall make all Europe quake. 156
   Third Mess. So you had need; for Orleans is be-
    sieg'd;
The English army is grown weak and faint;
The Earl of Salisbury craveth supply,
And hardly keeps his men from mutiny,   160
Since they, so few, watch such a multitude.
   Exe. Remember, lords, your oaths to Henry sworn,
Either to quell the Dauphin utterly,
Or bring him in obedience to your yoke.   164
   Bed. I do remember it; and here take my leave,
To go about my preparation.   *Exit Bedford.*
   Glo. I'll to the Tower with all the haste I can,
To view the artillery and munition;   168
And then I will proclaim young Henry king.
                      Exit Gloucester.
   Exe. To Eltham will I, where the young king is,
Being ordain'd his special governor;
And for his safety there I'll best devise.   *Exit.*
   Win. Each hath his place and function to at-
    tend: 173
I am left out; for me nothing remains.
But long I will not be Jack-out-of-office.
The king from Eltham I intend to steal,   176
And sit at chiefest stern of public weal.   *Exit.*

162 your oaths; *cf. n.*   163 quell: *destroy*   170 Eltham; *cf. n.*
177 at chiefest stern: *in supreme control*

Scene Two

[France.   Before Orleans]

Sound a Flourish.

*Enter Charles, Alençon, and Reignier, marching with
Drum and Soldiers.*

Char. Mars his true moving, even as in the heavens
So in the earth, to this day is not known.
Late did he shine upon the English side;
Now we are victors; upon us he smiles.   4
What towns of any moment but we have?
At pleasure here we lie near Orleans;
Otherwhiles the famish'd English, like pale ghosts,
Faintly besiege us one hour in a month.   8
   Alen. They want their porridge and their fat bull-
         beeves:
Either they must be dieted like mules
And have their provender tied to their mouths,
Or piteous they will look, like drowned mice.   12
   Reig. Let's raise the siege: why live we idly here?
Talbot is taken, whom we wont to fear:
Remaineth none but mad-brain'd Salisbury,
And he may well in fretting spend his gall;   16
Nor men nor money hath he to make war.
   Char. Sound, sound alarum! we will rush on them.
Now for the honour of the forlorn French!
Him I forgive my death that killeth me   20
When he sees me go back one foot or fly.   *Exeunt.*

*Here Alarum; they are beaten back by the English,
with great loss.*

Scene Two S. d. Flourish: *trumpet blast*
1 Mars his true moving: *Mars' exact movement; cf. n.*
7 Otherwhiles: *at times*   14 wont: *were wont*
17 Nor: *neither*   18 alarum: *call to arms*

Enter Charles, Alençon, and Reignier.

Char. Who ever saw the like? what men have I!
Dogs! cowards! dastards! I would ne'er have fled
But that they left me 'midst my enemies.   24
Reig. Salisbury is a desperate homicide;
He fighteth as one weary of his life:
The other lords, like lions wanting food,
Do rush upon us as their hungry prey.   28
Alen. Froissart, a countryman of ours, records,
England all Olivers and Rowlands bred
During the time Edward the Third did reign.
More truly now may this be verified;   32
For none but Samsons and Goliases
It sendeth forth to skirmish. One to ten!
Lean raw-bon'd rascals! who would e'er suppose
They had such courage and audacity?   36
   Char. Let's leave this town; for they are hare-
      brain'd slaves,
And hunger will enforce them to be more eager:
Of old I know them; rather with their teeth
The walls they'll tear down than forsake the siege. 40
   Reig. I think, by some odd gimmors or device,
Their arms are set like clocks, still to strike on;
Else ne'er could they hold out so as they do.
By my consent, we'll e'en let them alone.   44
   Alen. Be it so.

Enter the Bastard of Orleans.

Bast. Where's the prince Dauphin? I have news
   for him.
Char. Bastard of Orleans, thrice welcome to us.

28 hungry: *stimulating hunger*
30 Olivers and Rowlands: *knights like the best who followed Char*-
lemagne   33 Goliases: Goliaths (*Golias is the Latin form*)
41 gimmors: *mechanical joints*   42 still: *continually*

Bast. Methinks your looks are sad, your cheer
    appall'd:
Hath the late overthrow wrought this offence?
Be not dismay'd, for succour is at hand:
A holy maid hither with me I bring,
Which by a vision sent to her from heaven   52
Ordained is to raise this tedious siege,
And drive the English forth the bounds of France.
The spirit of deep prophecy she hath,
Exceeding the nine sibyls of old Rome;   56
What's past and what's to come she can descry.
Speak, shall I call her in?   Believe my words,
For they are certain and unfallible.
    Char. Go, call her in. [*Exit Bastard.*] But first, **to**
    try her skill,   60
Reignier, stand thou as Dauphin in my place:
Question her proudly; let thy looks be stern:
By this means shall we sound what skill she hath.

    Enter Joan Pucelle [*with Bastard*].

    Reig. Fair maid, is 't thou wilt do these wondrous
    feats?   64
    Joan. Reignier, is 't thou that thinkest to beguile
    me?
Where is the Dauphin?   Come, come from behind;
I know thee well, though never seen before.
Be not amaz'd, there's nothing hid from me: 68
In private will I talk with thee apart.
Stand back, you lords, and give us leave a while.
    Reig. She takes upon her bravely at first dash.
    Joan. Dauphin, I am by birth a shepherd's daugh-
    ter,   72
My wit untrain'd in any kind of art.

Heaven and our Lady gracious hath it pleas'd
To shine on my contemptible estate:
Lo! whilst I waited on my tender lambs,   76
And to sun's parching heat display'd my cheeks.
God's mother deigned to appear to me,
And in a vision full of majesty
Will'd me to leave my base vocation   80
And free my country from calamity:
Her aid she promis'd and assur'd success;
In complete glory she reveal'd herself;
And, whereas I was black and swart before,   84
With those clear rays which she infus'd on me,
That beauty am I bless'd with which you see.
Ask me what question thou canst possible
And I will answer unpremeditated: 88
My courage try by combat, if thou dar'st,
And thou shalt find that I exceed my sex.
Resolve on this, thou shalt be fortunate
If thou receive me for thy warlike mate.   92
    Char. Thou hast astonish'd me with thy high terms.
Only this proof I'll of thy valour make,
In single combat thou shalt buckle with me,
And if thou vanquishest, thy words are true;   96
Otherwise I renounce all confidence.
    Joan. I am prepar'd: here is my keen-edg'd sword,
Deck'd with five flower-de-luces on each side;
The which at Touraine, in Saint Katharine's church-
        yard,   100
Out of a great deal of old iron I chose forth.
    Char. Then come, o' God's name; I fear no woman.
    Joan. And, while I live, I'll ne'er fly from a man.
    Here they fight, and Joan la Pucelle overcomes.

93 high terms: *lofty language*   95 buckle: *contend*
99 Deck'd: *adorned*

Char. Stay, stay thy hands! thou art an Ama-
zon,   104
And fightest with the sword of Deborah.
   Joan. Christ's mother helps me, else I were too
weak.
   Char. Whoe'er helps thee, 'tis thou that must help
me:
Impatiently I burn with thy desire;   108
My heart and hands thou hast at once subdu'd.
Excellent Pucelle, if thy name be so,
Let me thy servant and not sovereign be;
'Tis the French Dauphin sueth to thee thus.   112
   Joan. I must not yield to any rites of love,
For my profession's sacred from above:
When I have chased all thy foes from hence,
Then will I think upon a recompense.   116
   Char. Meantime look gracious on thy prostrate
thrall.
   Reig. My lord, methinks, is very long in talk.
   Alen. Doubtless he shrives this woman to her
smock;
Else ne'er could he so long protract his speech.   120
   Reig. Shall we disturb him, since he keeps no
mean?
   Alen. He may mean more than we poor men do
know:
These women are shrewd tempters with their tongues.
   Reig. My lord, where are you? what devise you
on?   124
Shall we give over Orleans, or no?
   Joan. Why, no, I say, distrustful recreants!
Fight till the last gasp; I will be your guard.

105 sword of Deborah; *cf. n.*   110 Pucelle; *cf. n.*
121 mean: *moderation*

Char. What she says, I'll confirm: we'll fight it
out.   128
Joan. Assign'd am I to be the English scourge.
This night the siege assuredly I'll raise:
Expect Saint Martin's summer, halcyon days,
Since I have entered into these wars.   132
Glory is like a circle in the water,
Which never ceaseth to enlarge itself,
Till by broad spreading it disperse to nought.
With Henry's death the English circle ends;
Dispersed are the glories it included.   137
Now am I like that proud insulting ship
Which Cæsar and his fortune bare at once.
Char. Was Mahomet inspired with a dove?
Thou with an eagle art inspired then.   141
Helen, the mother of great Constantine,
Nor yet Saint Philip's daughters were like thee.
Bright star of Venus, fall'n down on the earth,
How may I reverently worship thee enough?
Alen. Leave off delays and let us raise the
siege.   146
Reig. Woman, do what thou canst to save our
honours;
Drive them from Orleans and be immortaliz'd.
Char. Presently we'll try. Come, let's away about
it:
No prophet will I trust if she prove false.   150

            Exeunt.

131 Saint Martin's summer; *cf. n.*   138, 139 *Cf. n.*
140 *Cf. n.*   142 *Cf. n.*   143 *Cf. n.*

Scene Three

[*London.   Before the Tower*]

Enter Gloucester, with his Serving-men [*in blue
coats*].

Glo. I am come to survey the Tower this day;
Since Henry's death, I fear, there is conveyance.
Where be these warders that they wait not here?
Open the gates! 'Tis Gloucester that calls.   4
                              [*Servants knock.*]
   First Ward. [*Within.*] Who's there that knocks so
   imperiously?
   First Serv. It is the noble Duke of Gloucester.
   Sec. Ward. [*Within.*] Whoe'er he be, you may not
   be let in.
   First Serv. Villains, answer you so the Lord Pro-
   tector?   8
   First Ward. [*Within.*] The Lord protect him! so
   we answer him:
We do not otherwise than we are will'd.
   Glo. Who willed you? or whose will stands but
   mine?
There's none protector of the realm but I.   12
Break up the gates, I'll be your warrantize:
Shall I be flouted thus by dunghill grooms?

*Gloucester's men rush at the Tower gates and Wood-
vile the Lieutenant speaks within.*

   Wood. What noise is this? what traitors have we
   here?
   Glo. Lieutenant, is it you whose voice I hear?
Open   the   gates!   here's   Gloucester   that   would
   enter.   17

2 conveyance: *underhand dealing*
13 Break up: *open forcibly*   warrantize: *surety*

Wood. [*Within.*] Have patience, noble **Duke; I**
  may not open,
The Cardinal of Winchester forbids:
From him I have express commandment   **20**
That thou nor none of thine shall be let in.
  Glo. Faint-hearted Woodvile, prizest him 'fore me?
Arrogant Winchester, that haughty prelate,
Whom Henry, our late sovereign, ne'er could
  brook?   **24**
Thou art no friend to God or to the king:
Open the gates, or I'll shut thee out shortly.
  First Serv. Open the gates unto the Lord Pro-
  tector;
Or we'll burst them open, if that you come not
  quickly.   **28**

*Enter to the Protector at the Tower gates Winchester
  and his men in tawny coats.*

  Win. How now, ambitious Humphrey! what means
  this?
  Glo. Peel'd priest, dost thou command me to be
  shut out?
  Win. I do, thou most usurping proditor.
And not protector, of the king or realm.   **32**
  Glo. Stand back, thou manifest conspirator,
Thou that contriv'dst to murder our dead lord;
Thou that giv'st whores indulgences to sin:
I'll canvass thee in thy broad cardinal's hat,   **3c**
If thou proceed in this thy insolence.
  Win. Nay, stand thou back; I will not budge a
  foot:

19 Cardinal; *cf. n.*   22 Woodvile; *cf. n.*
30 Peel'd: *tonsured*   31 proditor: *betrayer*
34 contriv'dst: *plottedst; cf. n.*   35 *Cf. n.*
36 canvass: *toss, as in a canvas sheet*

This be Damascus, be thou cursed Cain,
To slay thy brother Abel, if thou wilt.   40
    Glo. I will not slay thee, but I'll drive thee back:
Thy scarlet robes as a child's bearing-cloth
I'll use to carry thee out of this place.
    Win. Do what thou dar'st; I'll beard thee to thy
      face.   44
    Glo. What! am I dar'd and bearded to my face?—
Draw, men, for all this privileged place;
Blue coats to tawny coats. Priest, beware your
    beard;
I mean to tug it and to cuff you soundly.   48
Under my feet I stamp thy cardinal's hat:
In spite of pope or dignities of church,
Here by the cheeks I'll drag thee up and down.
    Win. Gloucester, thou'lt answer this before the
      pope.   52
    Glo. Winchester goose! I cry a rope! a rope!
Now beat them hence; why do you let them stay?
Thee I'll chase hence, thou wolf in sheep's array.
Out, tawny coats! out, scarlet hypocrite!   56
Here Gloucester's men beat out the Cardinal's men,
    and enter in the hurly-burly the Mayor of Lon-
    don and his Officers.
    May. Fie, lords! that you, being supreme magis-
      trates,
Thus contumeliously should break the peace!
    Glo. Peace, mayor! thou know'st little of my
      wrongs:
Here's Beaufort, that regards nor God nor King,
Hath here distrain'd the Tower to his use.   61
    Win. Here's Gloucester, a foe to citizens;

39 Damascus; *cf. n.*   42 bearing-cloth: *christening robe*
53 Winchester goose: *cant name of a foul disease*
61 distrain'd: *confiscated*

One that still motions war and never peace,
O'ercharging your free purses with large fines,   **64**
That seeks to overthrow religion
Because he is protector of the realm,
And would have armour here out of the Tower,
To crown himself king and suppress the prince.   **68**

    Glo. I will not answer thee with words, but blows.
                    Here they skirmish again.
    May. Nought rests for me, in this tumultuous
    strife
But to make open proclamation.
Come, officer: as loud as e'er thou canst;   **72**
Cry.

    Off. 'All manner of men, assembled here in
arms this day, against God's peace and the
king's, we charge and command you, in his highness' name, to repair to your several dwelling-
places; and not to wear, handle, or use, any
sword, weapon, or dagger, henceforward, upon
pain of death.'   **80**

    Glo. Cardinal, I'll be no breaker of the law;
But we shall meet and break our minds at large.

    Win. Gloucester, we will meet; to thy cost, be sure:
Thy heart-blood I will have for this day's work.

    May. I'll call for clubs if you will not away.
This cardinal's more haughty than the devil.   **86**

    Glo. Mayor, farewell: thou dost but what thou
    mayst.

    Win. Abominable Gloucester! guard thy head;
For I intend to have it ere long.

        Exeunt [*severally, Gloucester and Winchester,*
                    with their Serving-men].

63 motions: *advocates*   82 break: *express (with a pun)*
85 clubs: *the rallying cry to summon apprentices and other citizens*

May. See the coast clear'd, and then we will de-
part.   90
Good God! these nobles should such stomachs bear;
I myself fight not once in forty year.   *Exeunt.*

Scene Four

[France. Before Orleans]

Enter the Master-Gunner of Orleans and his Boy.

   M. Gun. Sirrah, thou know'st how Orleans is be-
     sieg'd,
And how the English have the suburbs won.
   Son. Father, I know; and oft have shot at them,
Howe'er unfortunate I miss'd my aim.   4
   M. Gun. But now thou shalt not. Be thou rul'd
     by me:
Chief master-gunner am I of this town;
Something I must do to procure me grace.
The prince's espials have informed me   8
How the English, in the suburbs close entrench'd,
Wont through a secret gate of iron bars
In yonder tower to overpeer the city,
And thence discover how with most **advantage**
They may vex us with shot or with assault.   13
To intercept this inconvenience,
A piece of ordnance 'gainst it I have plac'd;
And fully even these three days have I watch'd
If I could see them. Now, boy, do thou watch,   17
For I can stay no longer.
If thou spy'st any, run and bring me word;
And thou shalt find me at the Governor's.   *Exit.*
   Son. Father, I warrant you; take you no care;   21
I'll never trouble you if I may spy them.   *Exit.*

8 espials: *spies*   11 overpeer: *look down upon*

Enter Salisbury and Talbot on the turrets, with [Sir William Glansdale, Sir Thomas Gargrave, and] Others.

Sal. Talbot, my life, my joy! again return'd!
How wert thou handled being prisoner?   24
Or by what means got'st thou to be releas'd,
Discourse, I prithee, on this turret's top.
    Tal. The Duke of Bedford had a prisoner
Call'd the brave Lord Ponton de Santrailles;   28
For him I was exchang'd and ransomed.
But with a baser man at arms by far
Once in contempt they would have barter'd me:
Which I disdaining scorn'd, and craved death   32
Rather than I would be so vile-esteem'd.
In fine, redeem'd I was as I desir'd.
But, O! the treacherous Fastolfe wounds my heart:
Whom with my bare fists I would execute   36
If I now had him brought into my power.
    Sal. Yet tell'st thou not how thou wert entertain'd.
    Tal. With scoffs and scorns and contumelious taunts.
In open market-place produc'd they me,   40
To be a public spectacle to all:
Here, said they, is the terror of the French,
The scarecrow that affrights our children so.
Then broke I from the officers that led me,   44
And with my nails digg'd stones out of the ground
To hurl at the beholders of my shame.
My grisly countenance made others fly.
None durst come near for fear of sudden death.
In iron walls they deem'd me not secure;   49
So great fear of my name 'mongst them was spread
That they suppos'd I could rend bars of steel

23-56 *Cf. n.*   **33** entertain'd: *treated*

And spurn in pieces posts of adamant: 52
Wherefore a guard of chosen shot I had,
That walk'd about me every minute-while;
And if I did but stir out of my bed
Ready they were to shoot me to the heart.   56

Enter the Boy with a linstock.

Sal. I grieve to hear what torments you endur'd;
But we will be reveng'd sufficiently.
Now it is supper-time in Orleans:
Here, through this grate, I count each one,   60
And view the Frenchmen how they fortify:
Let us look in; the sight will much delight thee.
Sir Thomas Gargrave, and Sir William Glansdale,
Let me have your express opinions   64
Where is best place to make our battery next.
  Gar. I think at the north gate; for there stand
      lords.
  Glan. And I, here, at the bulwark of the bridge.
  Tal. For aught I see, this city must be famish'd, 68
Or with light skirmishes enfeebled.

*Here they shoot and Salisbury falls down
      [together with Gargrave].*

  Sal. O Lord! have mercy on us, wretched sinners.
  Gar. O Lord! have mercy on me, woeful man.
  Tal. What chance is this that suddenly hath
      cross'd us?   72
Speak, Salisbury; at least, if thou canst speak:
How far'st thou, mirror of all martial men?
One of thy eyes and thy cheek's side struck off!
Accursed tower! accursed fatal hand   76
That hath contriv'd this woeful tragedy!

53 chosen shot: *sharpshooters*
56 S. d. linstock: *stick holding gunner's match*
64 express: *precise*   68 must be: *will have to be*

In thirteen battles Salisbury o'ercame;
Henry the Fifth he first train'd to the wars;
Whilst any trump did sound or drum struck up,   80
His sword did ne'er leave striking in the field.
Yet liv'st thou, Salisbury? though thy speech doth
    fail,
One eye thou hast to look to heaven for grace:
The sun with one eye vieweth all the world.   84
Heaven, be thou gracious to none alive,
If Salisbury wants mercy at thy hands!
Bear hence his body; I will help to bury it.
Sir Thomas Gargrave, hast thou any life?   88
Speak unto Talbot; nay, look up to him.
Salisbury, cheer thy spirit with this comfort;
Thou shalt not die, whiles—
He beckons with his hand and smiles on me,   92
As who should say, 'When I am dead and gone,
Remember to avenge me on the French.'
Plantagenet, I will; and like thee,
Play on the lute, beholding the towns burn: 96
Wretched shall France be only in my name.
        Here an Alarum, and it thunders and lightens.
What stir is this? What tumult's in the heavens?
Whence cometh this alarum and the noise?

        Enter a Messenger.

    Mess. My lord, my lord! the French have gather'd
        head: 100
The Dauphin, with one Joan la Pucelle join'd,
A holy prophetess new risen up,
Is come with a great power to raise the siege.
        Here Salisbury lifteth himself up and groans.

81 leave: *cease from*
95 Plantagenet; *cf. n.*   like thee; *cf. n.*
97 only in: *at the mere sound of*   100 head: *armed force*

Tal. Hear,   hear   how   dying   Salisbury   doth
   groan!   104
It irks his heart he cannot be reveng'd.
Frenchmen, I'll be a Salisbury to you:
Pucelle or puzzel, dolphin or dogfish,
Your hearts I'll stamp out with my horse's heels
And make a quagmire of your mingled brains.
Convey me Salisbury into his tent,   110
And then we'll try what these dastard Frenchmen
   dare.
                   Alarum.   Exeunt [bearing out the bodies].

                        Scene Five

           [The Same.   Before one of the Gates]

*Here an Alarum again, and Talbot pursueth the
   Dauphin and driveth him.   Then enter Joan la
   Pucelle, driving Englishmen before her.   Then
   enter Talbot.*

   Tal. Where is my strength, my valour, and my
      force?
Our English troops retire, I cannot stay them;
A woman clad in armour chaseth them.

                   Enter Pucelle.

Here, here she comes.   I'll have a bout with thee:
Devil, or devil's dam, I'll conjure thee: 5
Blood will I draw on thee, thou art a witch,
And straightway give thy soul to him thou serv'st.
   Joan. Come, come; 'tis only I that must disgrace
      thee.   *Here they fight.*
   Tal. Heavens, can you suffer hell so to prevail?   9
My breast I'll burst with straining of my courage,

107 puzzel: *lewd woman*   dolphin or dogfish; *cf. n.*   6 *Cf. n.*

And from my shoulders crack my arms asunder,
But I will chastise this high-minded strumpet.   12
                              They fight again.
    Joan. Talbot, farewell; thy hour is not yet come:
I must go victual Orleans forthwith.
    A short Alarum; then [let Pucelle] enter the town
                              with Soldiers.
O'ertake me if thou canst; I scorn thy strength.
Go, go, cheer up thy hungry-starved men;   16
Help Salisbury to make his testament:
This day is ours, as many more shall be.   *Exit.*
    Tal. My thoughts are whirled like a potter's wheel;
I know not where I am, nor what I do: 20
A witch, by fear, not force, like Hannibal,
Drives back our troops and conquers as she lists:
So bees with smoke, and doves with noisome stench,
Are from their hives and houses driven away.   24
They call'd us for our fierceness English dogs;
Now, like to whelps, we crying run away.
                              A short Alarum.
Hark, countrymen! either renew the fight,
Or tear the lions out of England's coat;   28
Renounce your soil, give sheep in lions' stead:
Sheep run not half so treacherous from the wolf,
Or horse or oxen from the leopard,
As you fly from your oft-subdued slaves.   32
                    Alarum. Here another skirmish.
It will not be: retire into your trenches:
You all consented unto Salisbury's death,
For none would strike a stroke in his revenge.
Pucelle is entered into Orleans   36
In spite of us or aught that we could do.

12 high-minded: *presumptuous*   14 S. d. *Cf. n.*
21 like Hannibal; *cf. n.*   28 *Cf. n.*
29 give: *display (as a heraldic emblem)*

O! would I were to die with Salisbury.
The shame hereof will make me hide my head.

     Exit Talbot. Alarum, Retreat, Flourish.

Scene Six

[The Same]

*Enter, on the walls, Pucelle, Dauphin, Reignier,
Alençon, and Soldiers.*

 Joan. Advance our waving colours on the walls;
Rescu'd is Orleans from the English:
Thus Joan la Pucelle hath perform'd her word.
  Char. Divinest creature, Astræa's daughter,   4
How shall I honour thee for this success?
Thy promises are like Adonis' gardens,
That one day bloom'd and fruitful were the next.
France, triumph in thy glorious prophetess!   8
Recover'd is the town of Orleans:
More blessed hap did ne'er befall our state.
  Reig. Why ring not out the bells throughout the
  town?
Dauphin, command the citizens make bonfires   12
And feast and banquet in the open streets,
To celebrate the joy that God hath given us.
  Alen. All France will be replete with mirth and
  joy,
When they shall hear how we have play'd the men.   16
  Char. 'Tis Joan, not we, by whom the day is won;
For which I will divide my crown with her;
And all the priests and friars in my realm
Shall in procession sing her endless praise.   20

---

39 S. d. Retreat: *signal to recall troops*   1 Advance: *raise*
4 Astræa's daughter; *cf. n.*   6 Adonis' gardens; *cf. n.*

A statelier pyramis to her I'll rear
Than Rhodope's of Memphis ever was:
In memory of her when she is dead,
Her ashes, in an urn more precious   24
Than the rich-jewell'd coffer of Darius,
Transported shall be at high festivals
Before the kings and queens of France.
No longer on Saint Denis will we cry,   28
But Joan la Pucelle shall be France's saint.
Come in, and let us banquet royally,
After this golden day of victory.
                                        Flourish. Exeunt.

ACT SECOND

Scene One

[Before Orleans]

*Enter a [French] Sergeant of a Band, with two
                    Sentinels.*

Serg. Sirs, take your places and be vigilant.
If any noise or soldier you perceive
Near to the walls, by some apparent sign
Let us have knowledge at the court of guard.   4
    Sent. Sergeant, you shall.   *[Exit Sergeant.]*
                    Thus are poor servitors—
When others sleep upon their quiet beds—
Constrain'd to watch in darkness, rain, and cold.

*Enter Talbot, Bedford, and Burgundy, with [soldiers
    bearing] scaling-ladders; their drums beating a
    dead march.*

21 pyramis: *pyramid*   22 Rhodope's of Memphis; *cf. n.*
25 coffer of Darius; *cf. n.*   Act Second S. d. Band: *body of troops*
4 court of guard: *guardhouse*   7 S. d. dead march; *cf. n.*

Tal. Lord regent, and redoubted Burgundy,   8
By whose approach the regions of Artois,
Walloon, and Picardy, are friends to us,
This happy night the Frenchmen are secure,
Having all day carous'd and banqueted: 12
Embrace we then this opportunity,
As fitting best to quittance their deceit
Contriv'd by art and baleful sorcery.

 Bed. Coward of France! how much he wrongs his
  fame,   16
Despairing of his own arm's fortitude,
To join with witches and the help of hell!

 Bur. Traitors have never other company.
But what's that Pucelle whom they term so pure?

 Tal. A maid, they say.

 Bed.   A maid, and be so martial!   21

 Bur. Pray God she prove not masculine ere long;
If underneath the standard of the French
She carry armour, as she hath begun.   24

 Tal. Well, let them practise and converse with
  spirits;
God is our fortress, in whose conquering name
Let us resolve to scale their flinty bulwarks.

 Bed. Ascend, brave Talbot; we will follow
  thee.   28

 Tal. Not all together: better far, I guess,
That we do make our entrance several ways,
That if it chance the one of us do fail,
The other yet may rise against their force.   32

 Bed. Agreed. I'll to yond corner.

 Bur.   And I to this.

 Tal. And here will Talbot mount, or make his
  grave.

---

8 Burgundy; *cf. n.*   11 secure: *unsuspecting*
14 quittance: *requite* 25 practise: *conspire* 32 other: *others*

Now, Salisbury, for thee, and for the right
Of English Henry, shall this night appear   36
How much in duty I am bound to both.
    Sent. Arm, arm! the enemy doth make assault!

[*The English*] *cry, 'St. George!' 'A Talbot.' The
    French leap o'er the walls in their shirts. Enter,
    several ways, Bastard [of Orleans], Alençon,
    Reignier, half ready, and half unready.*

    Alen. How now, my lords! what! all unready so?
    Bast. Unready! ay, and glad we 'scap'd so well.
    Reig. 'Twas time, I trow, to wake and leave our
        beds,
Hearing alarums at our chamber-doors.
    Alen. Of all exploits since first I follow'd arms,
Ne'er heard I of a warlike enterprise   44
More venturous or desperate than this.
    Bast. I think this Talbot be a fiend of hell.
    Reig. If not of hell, the heavens, sure, favour him.
    Alen. Here cometh Charles: I marvel how he
        sped.   48
    Bast. Tut! holy Joan was his defensive guard.

                Enter Charles and Joan.

    Char. Is this thy cunning, thou deceitful dame?
Didst thou at first, to flatter us withal,
Make us partakers of a little gain,   52
That now our loss might be ten times so much?
    Joan. Wherefore is Charles impatient with his
        friend?
At all times will you have my power alike?
Sleeping or waking must I still prevail,   56
Or will you blame and lay the fault on me?

38 S. d. *Cf. n.*   39 unready: *undressed*

Improvident soldiers! had your watch been good,
This sudden mischief never could have fall'n.
   Char. Duke of Alençon, this was your default,
That, being captain of the watch to-night,   61
Did look no better to that weighty charge.
   Alen. Had all your quarters been so safely kept
As that whereof I had the government,   64
We had not been thus shamefully surpris'd.
   Bast. Mine was secure.
   Reig.   And so was mine, my lord.
   Char. And for myself, most part of all this night,
Within her quarter and mine own precinct   68
I was employ'd in passing to and fro,
About relieving of the sentinels:
Then how or which way should they first break in?
   Joan. Question, my lords, no further of the
      case,   72
How or which way: 'tis sure they found some place
But weakly guarded, where the breach was made.
And now there rests no other shift but this;
To gather our soldiers, scatter'd and dispers'd,
And lay new platforms to endamage them.   77

*Alarum.   Enter a Soldier, crying, 'A Talbot! a Tal-
   bot!'   They fly, leaving their clothes behind.*

   Sold. I'll be so bold to take what they have left.
The cry of Talbot serves me for a sword;
For I have loaden me with many spoils,   80
Using no other weapon but his name.   *Exit.*

68 her: *Joan's*   77 platforms: *plots*

Scene Two.

[Within the Town]

*Enter Talbot, Bedford, Burgundy [a Captain, and
Others].*

Bed. The day begins to break, and night is fled,
Whose pitchy mantle over-veil'd the earth.
Here sound retreat, and cease our hot pursuit.

                                        Retreat.

Tal. Bring forth the body of old Salisbury,   4
And here advance it in the market-place,
The middle centre of this cursed town.
Now have I paid my vow unto his soul;
For every drop of blood was drawn from him   8
There hath at least five Frenchmen died to-night.
And that hereafter ages may behold
What ruin happen'd in revenge of him,
Within their chiefest temple I'll erect   12
A tomb wherein his corse shall be interr'd:
Upon the which, that every one may read,
Shall be engrav'd the sack of Orleans,
The treacherous manner of his mournful death,
And what a terror he had been to France.   17
But, lords, in all our bloody massacre,
I muse we met not with the Dauphin's grace,
His new-come champion, virtuous Joan of Arc,
Nor any of his false confederates.   21
  Bed. 'Tis thought, Lord Talbot, when the fight
      began,
Rous'd on the sudden from their drowsy beds,
They did amongst the troops of armed men   24
Leap o'er the walls for refuge in the field.
  Bur. Myself—as far as I could well discern

8 was: *which was*   19 muse: *wonder*

For smoke and dusky vapours of the night—
Am sure I scar'd the Dauphin and his trull,   28
When arm in arm they both came swiftly running,
Like to a pair of loving turtle-doves
That could not live asunder day or night.
After that things are set in order here,   32
We'll follow them with all the power we have.

Enter a Messenger.

  Mess. All hail, my lords! Which of this princely train
Call ye the warlike Talbot, for his acts
So much applauded through the realm of France?   36
  Tal. Here is the Talbot: who would speak with him?
  Mess. The virtuous lady, Countess of Auvergne,
With modesty admiring thy renown,
By me entreats, great lord, thou wouldst vouch-
    safe   40
To visit her poor castle where she lies,
That she may boast she hath beheld the man
Whose glory fills the world with loud report.
  Bur. Is it even so? Nay, then, I see our wars
Will turn into a peaceful comic sport,   45
When ladies crave to be encounter'd with.
You may not, my lord, despise her gentle suit.
  Tal. Ne'er trust me then; for when a world of men   48
Could not prevail with all their oratory,
Yet hath a woman's kindness over-rul'd:
And therefore tell her I return great thanks,
And in submission will attend on her.   52
Will not your honours bear me company?

41 lies: *dwells*

Bed. No, truly; 'tis more than manners will;
And I have heard it said, unbidden guests
Are often welcomest when they are gone.   56
   Tal. Well then, alone,—since there's no remedy,—
I mean to prove this lady's courtesy.
Come hither. captain.   *Whispers.*
                    You perceive my mind.
   Capt. I do, my lord, and mean accordingly.
                                     Exeunt.

                    Scene Three.

          [*Auvergne. Court of the Castle*]

          Enter Countess [and her Porter].

   Count. Porter, remember what I gave in charge;
And when you have done so, bring the keys to me.
   Port. Madam, I will.   *Exit.*
   Count. The plot is laid: if all things fall out
      right,   4
I shall as famous be by this exploit
As Scythian Tomyris by Cyrus' death.
Great is the rumour of this dreadful knight,
And his achievements of no less account: 8
Fain would mine eyes be witness with mine ears,
To give their censure of these rare reports.

          Enter a Messenger and Talbot.

   Mess. Madam,
According as your ladyship desir'd,   12
By message crav'd, so is Lord Talbot come.
   Count. And he is welcome. What! is this the man?
   Mess. Madam, it is.

6 **Scythian Tomyris:** *cf. a.*   10 censure: *opinion*

Count. Is this the scourge of France?
Is this the Talbot, so much fear'd abroad, 16
That with his name the mothers still their babes?
I see report is fabulous and false:
I thought I should have seen some Hercules,
A second Hector, for his grim aspect, 20
And large proportion of his strong-knit limbs.
Alas! this is a child, a silly dwarf:
It cannot be this weak and writhled shrimp
Should strike such terror to his enemies. 24

Tal. Madam, I have been bold to trouble you;
But since your ladyship is not at leisure,
I'll sort some other time to visit you.

Count. What means he now? Go ask him whither
he goes. 28

Mess. Stay, my Lord Talbot; for my lady craves
To know the cause of your abrupt departure.

Tal. Marry, for that she's in a wrong belief,
I go to certify her Talbot's here. 32

Enter Porter, with keys.

Count. If thou be he, then art thou prisoner.
Tal. Prisoner! to whom?
Count. To me, bloodthirsty lord;
And for that cause I train'd thee to my house.
Long time thy shadow hath been thrall to me, 36
For in my gallery thy picture hangs:
But now the substance shall endure the like,
And I will chain these legs and arms of thine,
That hast by tyranny, these many years, 40
Wasted our country, slain our citizens,
And sent our sons and husbands captivate.

Tal. Ha, ha, ha!

22 *Cf. n.* 23 writhled: *wrinkled* 27 sort: *choose*
32 certify: *inform* 35 train'd: *lured* 42 captivate: *into captivity*

Count. Laughest thou, wretch? thy mirth shall
   turn to moan.   **44**
Tal. I laugh to see your ladyship so fond
To think that you have aught but Talbot's shadow,
Whereon to practise your severity.
  Count. Why, art not thou the man?
  Tal.   I am, indeed. **48**
  Count. Then have I substance too.
  Tal. No, no, I am but shadow of myself:
You are deceiv'd, my substance is not here;
For what you see is but the smallest part   **52**
And least proportion of humanity.
I tell you, madam, were the whole frame here,
It is of such a spacious lofty pitch,
Your roof were not sufficient to contain it.   **56**
  Count. This is a riddling merchant for the nonce;
He will be here, and yet he is not here:
How can these contrarieties agree?
  Tal. That will I show you presently.   **60**

Winds his horn. Drums strike up; a peal of ord-
       nance. Enter Soldiers.

How say you, madam? are you now persuaded
That Talbot is but shadow of himself?
These are his substance, sinews, arms, and strength,
With which he yoketh your rebellious necks,   **64**
Razeth your cities, and subverts your towns,
And in a moment makes them desolate.
  Count. Victorious Talbot! pardon my abuse:
I find thou art no less than fame hath bruited,   **68**
And more than may be gather'd by thy shape.
Let my presumption not provoke thy wrath;
For I am sorry that with reverence

45 fond: *foolish*   55 pitch: *height*
57 riddling merchant: *riddle-monger*   60 presently: *immediately*

I did not entertain thee as thou art.   72

   Tal. Be not dismay'd, fair lady; nor misconster
The mind of Talbot as you did mistake
The outward composition of his body.
What you have done hath not offended me;   76
Nor other satisfaction do I crave,
But only, with your patience, that we may
Taste of your wine and see what cates you have;
For soldiers' stomachs always serve them well.

   Count. With all my heart, and think me hon-
     oured   81
To feast so great a warrior in my house.   *Exeunt.*

Scene Four.

[*London.   The Temple Garden*]

Enter Richard Plantagenet, Warwick, Somerset, Pole
   [Earl of Suffolk], and others [Vernon and a
   Lawyer].

   Plan. Great lords, and gentlemen, what means this
     silence?
Dare no man answer in a case of truth?

   Suf. Within the Temple hall we were too loud;
The garden here is more convenient.   4

   Plan. Then say at once if I maintain'd the truth,
Or else was wrangling Somerset in th' error?

   Suf. Faith, I have been a truant in the law,
And never yet could frame my will to it;   8
And therefore frame the law unto my will.

   Som. Judge you, my Lord of Warwick, then, be-
     tween us.

73 misconster: *misconstrue*   79 cates: *delicacies*   6 Cf. *n.*   7 *Cf.* &c.

War. Between two hawks, which flies the higher
    pitch;
Between two dogs, which hath the deeper mouth;
Between two blades, which bears the better tem-
    per; 13
Between two horses, which doth bear him best;
Between two girls, which hath the merriest eye;
I have perhaps some shallow spirit of judgment; 16
But in these nice sharp quillets of the law,
Good faith, I am no wiser than a daw.
    Plan. Tut, tut! here is a mannerly forbearance:
The truth appears so naked on my side, 20
That any purblind eye may find it out.
    Som. And on my side it is so well apparell'd,
So clear, so shining, and so evident,
That it will glimmer through a blind man's eye. 24
    Plan. Since you are tongue-tied, and so loath to
    speak,
In dumb significants proclaim your thoughts:
Let him that is a true-born gentleman,
And stands upon the honour of his birth, 28
If he suppose that I have pleaded truth,
From off this brier pluck a white rose with me.
    Som. Let him that is no coward nor no flatterer,
But dare maintain the party of the truth, 32
Pluck a red rose from off this thorn with me.
    War. I love no colours, and, without all colour
Of base insinuating flattery
I pluck this white rose with Plantagenet. 36
    Suf. I pluck this red rose with young Somerset:
And say withal I think he held the right.
    Ver. Stay, lords and gentlemen, and pluck no more,

17 quillets: *subtleties*   26 significants: *signs*   32 party: *side*
34 colours: *pun on meaning, 'pretences'*
36 Plantagenet; *cf. n. on I. iv. 95*

Till you conclude that he, upon whose side   40
The fewest roses are cropp'd from the tree,
Shall yield the other in the right opinion.
 Som. Good Master Vernon, it is well objected:
If I have fewest I subscribe in silence.   44
 Plan. And I.
 Ver. Then for the truth and plainness of the case,
I pluck this pale and maiden blossom here,
Giving my verdict on the white rose side.   48
 Som. Prick not your finger as you pluck it off,
Lest bleeding you do paint the white rose red,
And fall on my side so, against your will.
 Ver. If I, my lord, for my opinion bleed,   52
Opinion shall be surgeon to my hurt,
And keep me on the side where still I am.
 Som. Well, well, come on: who else?
 Lawyer. [*To Somerset.*] Unless my study and my
  books be false,   56
The argument you held was wrong in you,
In sign whereof I pluck a white rose too.
 Plan. Now, Somerset, where is your argument?
 Som. Here, in my scabbard; meditating that   60
Shall dye your white rose in a bloody red.
 Plan. Meantime, your cheeks do counterfeit our
  roses;
For pale they look with fear, as witnessing
The truth on our side.
 Som.   No, Plantagenet,   64
'Tis not for fear but anger that thy cheeks
Blush for pure shame to counterfeit our roses,
And yet thy tongue will not confess thy error.
 Plan. Hath not thy rose a canker, Somerset?

43 objected: *proposed*   44 subscribe: *submit*
68 canker: *canker-worm*

Som. Hath not thy rose a thorn, Plantagenet? 69
Plan. Ay, sharp and piercing, to maintain his
truth;
Whiles thy consuming canker eats his falsehood.
Som. Well, I'll find friends to wear my bleeding
roses, 72
That shall maintain what I have said is true,
Where false Plantagenet dare not be seen.
Plan. Now, by this maiden blossom in my hand,
I scorn thee and thy faction, peevish boy. 76
Suf. Turn not thy scorns this way, Plantagenet.
Plan. Proud Pole, I will, and scorn both him and
thee.
Suf. I'll turn my part thereof into thy throat.
Som. Away, away! good William de la Pole: 80
We grace the yeoman by conversing with him.
War. Now, by God's will, thou wrong'st him,
Somerset:
His grandfather was Lionel, Duke of Clarence,
Third son to the third Edward, King of England. 84
Spring crestless yeomen from so deep a root?
Plan. He bears him on the place's privilege,
Or durst not, for his craven heart, say thus.
Som. By Him that made me, I'll maintain my
words 88
On any plot of ground in Christendom.
Was not thy father, Richard Earl of Cambridge,
For treason executed in our late king's days?
And, by his treason stand'st not thou attainted,
Corrupted, and exempt from ancient gentry?
His trespass yet lives guilty in thy blood; 94
And, till thou be restor'd, thou art a yeoman.

81 the yeoman; *cf. n.*   86 bears him on: *takes advantage of*
93 exempt: *cut off*

Plan. My father was attached, not attainted;
Condemn'd to die for treason, but no traitor;
And that I'll prove on better men than Somerset,
Were growing time once ripen'd to my will.
For your partaker Pole and you yourself,   100
I'll note you in my book of memory,
To scourge you for this apprehension:
Look to it well and say you are well warn'd.
    Som. Ah, thou shalt find us ready for thee still, 104
And know us by these colours for thy foes;
For these my friends in spite of thee shall wear.
    Plan. And, by my soul, this pale and angry rose,
As cognizance of my blood-drinking hate,   108
Will I for ever and my faction wear,
Until it wither with me to my grave
Or flourish to the height of my degree.
    Suf. Go forward, and be chok'd with thy ambi-
      tion: 112
And so farewell until I meet thee next.   *Exit.*
    Som. Have with thee, Pole. Farewell, ambitious
      Richard.   *Exit.*
    Plan. How I am brav'd and must perforce endure
      it!
    War. This blot that they object against your
      house   116
Shall be wip'd out in the next parliament,
Call'd for the truce of Winchester and Gloucester;
And if thou be not then created York,
I will not live to be accounted Warwick.   120
Meantime in signal of my love to thee,
Against proud Somerset and William Pole,
Will I upon thy party wear this rose.

96 attached, not attainted; *cf. n.*   100 partaker: *supporter*
102 apprehension: *conception, opinion*   111 degree: *rank*
114 Have with thee: *let us go*

And here I prophesy: this brawl to-day,   124
Grown to this faction in the Temple garden,
Shall send between the red rose and the white
A thousand souls to death and deadly night.
    Plan. Good Master Vernon, I am bound **to**
      you,   128
That you on my behalf would pluck a flower.
    Ver. In your behalf still would I wear the same.
    Lawyer. And so will I.
    Plan. Thanks, gentle sir.   132
Come, let us four to dinner: I dare say
This quarrel will drink blood another day,   *Exeunt.*

Scene Five

[London.   A Room in the Tower]

Enter Mortimer, brought in a chair, and Jailors.

    Mor. Kind keepers of my weak decaying age,
Let dying Mortimer here rest himself.
Even like a man new haled from the rack,
So fare my limbs with long imprisonment;   4
And these gray locks, the pursuivants of death,
Nestor-like aged, in an age of care,
Argue the end of Edmund Mortimer.
These eyes, like lamps whose wasting oil is spent,   8
Wax dim, as drawing to their exigent;
Weak shoulders, overborne with burdening grief,
And pithless arms, like to a wither'd vine
That droops his sapless branches to the ground: 12
Yet are these feet whose strengthless stay is numb,
Unable to support this lump of clay,

5 pursuivants: *messengers*   6 *Cf. n.*
7 Edmund Mortimer; *cf. n.*   9 exigent: *end*

Swift-winged with desire to get a grave,
As witting I no other comfort have.   16
But tell me, keeper, will my nephew come?
   First Keep. Richard Plantagenet, my lord, will
    come:
We sent unto the Temple, unto his chamber,
And answer was return'd that he will come.   20
   Mor. Enough: my soul shall then be satisfied.
Poor gentleman! his wrong doth equal mine.
Since Henry Monmouth first began to reign,
Before whose glory I was great in arms,   24
This loathsome sequestration have I had;
And even since then hath Richard been obscur'd,
Depriv'd of honour and inheritance.
But now the arbitrator of despairs,   28
Just death, kind umpire of men's miseries,
With sweet enlargement doth dismiss me hence:
I would his troubles likewise were expir'd,
That so he might recover what was lost.   32

              Enter Richard.

   First Keep. My lord, your loving nephew now is
    come.
   Mor. Richard Plantagenet, my friend, is he come?
   Plan. Ay, noble uncle, thus ignobly us'd,
Your nephew, late despised Richard, comes.   36
   Mor. Direct mine arms I may embrace his neck,
And in his bosom spend my latter gasp:
O! tell me when my lips do touch his cheeks,
That I may kindly give one fainting kiss.   40
And now declare, sweet stem from York's great stock,
Why didst thou say of late thou wert despis'd?
   Plan. First, lean thine aged back against mine arm;

25 sequestration: *seclusion, imprisonment*   38 latter: *final*

And in that ease, I'll tell thee my disease.   44
This day, in argument upon a case,
Some words there grew 'twixt Somerset and me;
Among which terms he us'd a lavish tongue
And did upbraid me with my father's death: 48
Which obloquy set bars before my tongue,
Else with the like I had requited him.
Therefore, good uncle, for my father's sake,
In honour of a true Plantagenet,   52
And for alliance sake, declare the cause
My father, Earl of Cambridge, lost his head.
    Mor. That cause, fair nephew, that imprison'd me,
And hath detain'd me all my flow'ring youth   56
Within a loathsome dungeon, there to pine,
Was cursed instrument of his decease.
    Plan. Discover more at large what cause that was,
For I am ignorant and cannot guess.   60
    Mor. I will, if that my fading breath permit,
And death approach not ere my tale be done.
Henry the Fourth, grandfather to this king,
Depos'd his nephew Richard, Edward's son,   64
The first-begotten, and the lawful heir
Of Edward king, the third of that descent:
During whose reign the Percies of the North,
Finding his usurpation most unjust,   68
Endeavour'd my advancement to the throne.
The reason mov'd these warlike lords to this
Was, for that—young Richard thus remov'd,
Leaving no heir begotten of his body—   72
I was the next by birth and parentage;
For by my mother I derived am

44 disease: *grievance*   53 alliance sake: *sake of relationship*
59 Discover: *make known*
64 nephew: *blood relative, here first cousin*
67 whose: *Henry IV's*   74 mother: *i.e., paternal grandmother*

From Lionel Duke of Clarence, the third son
To King Edward the Third; whereas he   76
From John of Gaunt doth bring his pedigree,
Being but fourth of that heroic line.
But mark: as, in this haughty great attempt
They laboured to plant the rightful heir,   80
I lost my liberty, and they their lives.
Long after this, when Henry the Fifth,
Succeeding his father Bolingbroke, did reign,
Thy father, Earl of Cambridge, then deriv'd   84
From famous Edmund Langley, Duke of York,
Marrying my sister that thy mother was,
Again in pity of my hard distress
Levied an army, weening to redeem   88
And have install'd me in the diadem;
But, as the rest, so fell that noble earl,
And was beheaded.   Thus the Mortimers,
In whom the title rested, were suppress'd.   92
    Plan. Of which, my lord, your honour is the last.
    Mor. True; and thou seest that I no issue have,
And that my fainting words do warrant death:
Thou art my heir; the rest I wish thee gather: 96
But yet be wary in thy studious care.
    Plan. Thy grave admonishments prevail with me.
But yet methinks my father's execution
Was nothing less than bloody tyranny.   100
    Mor. With silence, nephew, be thou politic:
Strong-fixed is the house of Lancaster,
And like a mountain, not to be remov'd.
But now thy uncle is removing hence,   104
As princes do their courts, when they are cloy'd
With long continuance in a settled place.
    Plan. O uncle! would some part of my young years

95 warrant: *certify*   96 the rest . . . gather; *cf. n.*

Might but redeem the passage of your age.   108
   Mor. Thou dost then wrong me,—as the slaugh-
    terer doth,
Which giveth many wounds when one will kill.—
Mourn not, except thou sorrow for my good;
Only give order for my funeral: 112
And so farewell; and fair be all thy hopes,
And prosperous be thy life in peace and war!
                        Dies.

   Plan. And peace, no war, befall thy parting soul!
In prison hast thou spent a pilgrimage,   116
And like a hermit overpass'd thy days.
Well, I will lock his counsel in my breast;
And what I do imagine let that rest.
Keepers, convey him hence; and I myself   120
Will see his burial better than his life.
         Exeunt [*Jailors, bearing out the body of*
                         Mortimer].
Here dies the dusky torch of Mortimer,
Chok'd with ambition of the meaner sort:
And, for those wrongs, those bitter injuries,   124
Which Somerset hath offer'd to my house,
I doubt not but with honour to redress;
And therefore haste I to the parliament,
Either to be restored to my blood,   128
Or make my ill the advantage of my good.   *Exit.*

128 blood: *hereditary rights*   129 *Cf. n.*

ACT THIRD

Scene One

[London. The Parliament House]

Flourish. Enter King, Exeter, Gloucester, Winches-
ter, Warwick, Somerset, Suffolk, Richard Plan-
tagenet. Gloucester offers to put up a bill;
Winchester snatches it, tears it.

Win. Com'st thou with deep premeditated lines,
With written pamphlets studiously devis'd,
Humphrey of Gloucester? If thou canst accuse,
Or aught intend'st to lay unto my charge,　　　　4
Do it without invention, suddenly;
As I, with sudden and extemporal speech
Purpose to answer what thou canst object.
　　Glo. Presumptuous priest! this place commands my
　　　　patience　　　　　　　　　　　　　　　　8
Or thou shouldst find thou hast dishonour'd me.
Think not, although in writing I preferr'd
The manner of thy vile outrageous crimes,
That therefore I have forg'd, or am not able　　12
Verbatim to rehearse the method of my pen:
No, prelate; such is thy audacious wickedness,
Thy lewd, pestiferous, and dissentious pranks,
As very infants prattle of thy pride.　　　　16
Thou art a most pernicious usurer,
Froward by nature, enemy to peace;
Lascivious, wanton, more than well beseems
A man of thy profession and degree;　　　　26
And for thy treachery, what's more manifest,

Act Third, Scene One; *cf. n.*　　　　5 invention: *preconceived design*
9 find: *i.e., to thy sorrow*
13 method . . . pen: *summary of what I have written*

In that thou laid'st a trap to take my life
As well at London Bridge as at the Tower?
Beside, I fear me, if thy thoughts were sifted,   **24**
The king, thy sovereign, is not quite exempt
From envious malice of thy swelling heart.
　　Win. Gloucester, I do defy thee. Lords, vouchsafe
To give me hearing what I shall reply.   **28**
If I were covetous, ambitious, or perverse,
As he will have me, how am I so poor?
Or how haps it I seek not to advance
Or raise myself, but keep my wonted calling?   **32**
And for dissension, who preferreth peace
More than I do, except I be provok'd?
No, my good lords, it is not that offends;
It is not that that hath incens'd the duke: **36**
It is, because no one should sway but he;
No one but he should be about the king;
And that engenders thunder in his breast,
And makes him roar these accusations forth.   **40**
But he shall know I am as good—
　　Glo.　　　　　　　　　　As good!
Thou bastard of my grandfather!
　　Win. Ay, lordly sir; for what are you, I pray,
But one imperious in another's throne?   **44**
　　Glo. Am I not protector, saucy priest?
　　Win. And am not I a prelate of the church?
　　Glo. Yes, as an outlaw in a castle keeps,
And useth it to patronage his theft.   **48**
　　Win. Unreverent Gloucester!
　　Glo.　　　　　　　　　Thou art reverent,
Touching thy spiritual function, not thy life.

22, 23 *Cf. n.*　　　　　　44 imperious: *playing the emperor*
48 patronage: *maintain, dignify*　　　49 reverent: *reverend*

Win. Rome shall remedy this.

War.   Roam thither then.

Som. My lord, it were your duty to forbear.   52

War. Ay, see the bishop be not overborne.

Som. Methinks my lord should be religious,
And know the office that belongs to such.

War. Methinks his lordship should be humbler;   56
It fitteth not a prelate so to plead.

Som. Yes, when his holy state is touch'd so near.

War. State holy, or unhallow'd, what of that?
Is not his Grace protector to the king?   60

Plan. [*Aside.*] Plantagenet, I see, must hold his
      tongue,
Lest it be said, 'Speak, sirrah, when you should;
Must your bold verdict enter talk with lords?'
Else would I have a fling at Winchester.   64

King. Uncles of Gloucester and of Winchester,
The special watchmen of our English weal,
I would prevail, if prayers might prevail,
To join your hearts in love and amity.   68
O! what a scandal is it to our crown,
That two such noble peers as ye should jar.
Believe me, lords, my tender years can tell
Civil dissension is a viperous worm,   72
That gnaws the bowels of the commonwealth.

            A noise within; 'Down with the tawny-coats!'

King. What tumult's this?

War.   An uproar, I dare warrant,
Begun through malice of the bishop's men.

                A noise again; 'Stones! Stones!'

Enter Mayor [*of London*].

May. O, my good lords, and virtuous Henry,   76

52 *Cf.* **n.**   63 enter talk; *cf.* **n.**

Pity the city of London, pity us!
The bishop and the Duke of Gloucester's men,
Forbidden late to carry any weapon,
Have fill'd their pockets full of pebble stones, 80
And banding themselves in contrary parts
Do pelt so fast at one another's pate,
That many have their giddy brains knock'd out:
Our windows are broke down in every street, 84
And we for fear compell'd to shut our shops.

*Enter, in skirmish, [the Serving-men of Gloucester
  and Winchester] with bloody pates.*

 King. We charge you, on allegiance to ourself,
To hold your slaught'ring hands, and keep the
  peace.—·
Pray, uncle Gloucester, mitigate this strife. 88
 First Serv. Nay, if we be forbidden stones,
we'll fall to it with our teeth.
 Sec. Serv. Do what ye dare, we are as resolute.
          Skirmish again.
 Glo. You of my household, leave this peevish
  broil, 92
And set this unaccustom'd fight aside.
 Third Serv. My lord, we know your Grace to be a
  man
Just and upright, and, for your royal birth,
Inferior to none but to his majesty; 96
And ere that we will suffer such a prince,
So kind a father of the commonweal,
To be disgraced by an inkhorn mate,
We and our wives and children all will fight, 100
And have our bodies slaught'red by thy foes.
 First Serv. Ay, and the very parings of our nails

78-85 *Cf. n.*   99 inkhorn mate: *low pedant*

Shall pitch a field when we are dead.   *Begin again.*
  Glo.   Stay, stay, I say!
And, if you love me, as you say you do,   104
Let me persuade you to forbear a while.
  King. O! how this discord doth afflict my soul!
Can you, my Lord of Winchester, behold
My sighs and tears and will not once relent?   108
Who should be pitiful if you be not?
Or who should study to prefer a peace
If holy churchmen take delight in broils?
  War. Yield, my Lord Protector; yield, Win-
    chester;   112
Except you mean with obstinate repulse
To slay your sovereign and destroy the realm.
You see what mischief and what murder too
Hath been enacted through your enmity: 116
Then be at peace, except ye thirst for blood.
  Win. He shall submit or I will never yield.
  Glo. Compassion on the king commands me stoop;
Or I would see his heart out ere the priest   120
Should ever get that privilege of me.
  War. Behold, my Lord of Winchester, the duke
Hath banish'd moody discontented fury,
As by his smoothed brows it doth appear: 124
Why look you still so stern and tragical?
  Glo. Here, Winchester, I offer thee my hand.
  King. Fie, uncle Beaufort! I have heard you
    preach,
That malice was a great and grievous sin;   128
And will not you maintain the thing you teach,
But prove a chief offender in the same?
  War. Sweet king! the bishop hath a kindly gird.

103 pitch a field: *do battle*   121 privilege: *advantage*
131 gird: *rebuke*

For shame, my Lord of Winchester, relent!   132
What! shall a child instruct you what to do?
> *Win.* Well, Duke of Gloucester, I will yield to
> thee;
Love for thy love and hand for hand I give.
> *Glo.* [*Aside.*] Ay; but I fear me, with a hollow
> heart.   136
See here, my friends and loving countrymen,
This token serveth for a flag of truce,
Betwixt ourselves and all our followers.
So help me God, as I dissemble not!   140
> *Win.* [*Aside.*] So help me God, as I intend it not!
> *King.* O loving uncle, kind Duke of Gloucester,
How joyful am I made by this contract!
Away, my masters! trouble us no more;   144
But join in friendship, as your lords have done.
> *First Serv.* Content: I'll to the surgeon's.
> *Sec. Serv.*   And so will I
> *Third Serv.* And I will see what physic the tavern
> affords.
>   *Exeunt* [*Mayor, Serving-men, &c.*].
> *War.* Accept this scroll, most gracious sove-
> reign,   148
Which in the right of Richard Plantagenet
We do exhibit to your majesty.
> *Glo.* Well urg'd, my Lord of Warwick: for, sweet
> prince,
An if your Grace mark every circumstance,   152
You have great reason to do Richard right;
Especially for those occasions
At Eltham-place I told your majesty.
> *King.* And those occasions, uncle, were of
> force: 156

144 my masters: *good fellows (a term of condescension)*
152 An if: *if*   154 occasions: *reasons*

Therefore, my loving lords, our pleasure is
That Richard be restored to his blood.
    War. Let Richard be restored to his blood;
So shall his father's wrongs be recompens'd.   160
    Win. As will the rest, so willeth Winchester.
    King. If Richard will be true, not that alone,
But all the whole inheritance I give
That doth belong unto the house of York,   164
From whence you spring by lineal descent.
    Plan. Thy humble servant vows obedience,
And humble service till the point of death.
    King. Stoop then and set your knee against my
        foot;   168
And, in reguerdon of that duty done,
I girt thee with the valiant sword of York:
Rise, Richard, like a true Plantagenet,
And rise created princely Duke of York.   172
    Plan. And so thrive Richard as thy foes may fall!
And as my duty springs, so perish they
That grudge one thought against your majesty!
    All. Welcome, high prince, the mighty Duke of
        York!   176
    Som. [*Aside.*] Perish, base prince, ignoble Duke of
        York!
    Glo. Now will it best avail your majesty
To cross the seas and to be crown'd in France.
The presence of a king engenders love   180
Amongst his subjects and his loyal friends,
As it disanimates his enemies.
    King. When Gloucester says the word, King Henry
        goes;
For friendly counsel cuts off many foes.   184

163-165 *Cf. n.*   169 reguerdon: *reward*   170 girt: *gird*
175 grudge . . . thought: *bear . . . grudging thought*
178, 179 *Cf. n.*   182 disanimates: *discourage*

Glo. Your ships already are in readiness.
                    Sennet. Flourish. Exeunt.

                    Manet Exeter.

Exe. Ay, we may march in England or in France,
Not seeing what is likely to ensue.
This late dissension grown betwixt the peers   188
Burns under feigned ashes of forg'd love,
And will at last break out into a flame:
As fester'd members rot but by degree,
Till bones and flesh and sinews fall away,   192
So will this base and envious discord breed.
And now I fear that fatal prophecy
Which in the time of Henry, nam'd the Fifth,
Was in the mouth of every sucking babe: 196
That Henry born at Monmouth should win all,
And Henry born at Windsor lose all:
Which is so plain that Exeter doth wish
His days may finish ere that hapless time.   200
                                            Exit.

                    Scene Two

              [*France.   Before Rouen*]

*Enter Pucelle, disguised, with four Soldiers [dressed
like countrymen,] with sacks upon their backs.*

Joan. These are the city gates, the gates of Roan,
Through which our policy must make a breach:
Take heed, be wary how you place your words;
Talk like the vulgar sort of market-men   4
That come to gather money for their corn.
If we have entrance,—as I hope we shall,—

And that we find the slothful watch but weak,
I'll by a sign give notice to our friends,   8
That Charles the Dauphin may encounter them.

 First Sold. Our sacks shall be a mean to sack the
  city,
And we be lords and rulers over Roan;
Therefore we'll knock.   *Knock.*

 Watch. [*Within.*] *Qui est là?*   13

 Joan. Paysans, pauvres gens de France:
Poor market-folks that come to sell their corn.

 Watch. [*Opening the gates.*] Enter, go in; the
  market-bell is rung.   16

 Joan. Now, Roan, I'll shake thy bulwarks to the
  ground. *Exeunt* [*Pucelle, &c., into the city*].

 Enter Charles, Bastard, Alençon [*and Forces*].

 Char. Saint Denis bless this happy stratagem!
And once again we'll sleep secure in Roan.

 Bast. Here enter'd Pucelle and her practis-
  ants;   20
Now she is there how will she specify
Where is the best and safest passage in?

 Alen. By thrusting out a torch from yonder tower;
Which, once discern'd, shows that her meaning is,   24
No way to that, for weakness, which she enter'd.

 Enter Pucelle on the top, thrusting out a torch
     burning.

 Joan. Behold! this is the happy wedding torch
That joineth Roan unto her countrymen,   27
But burning fatal to the Talbonites! [*Exit.*]

 Bast. See, noble Charles, the beacon of our friend,

7 that: *i.e., if* 16 market-bell: *bell signaling the opening of market*
20 practisants: *conspirators*   22 Where; *cf. n.*
25 to: *is comparable to*   28 Talbonites; *cf. n.*

The burning torch in yonder turret stands.
   Char. Now shine it like a comet of revenge,
A prophet to the fall of all our foes!   32
   Alen. Defer no time, delays have dangerous ends;
Enter, and cry 'The Dauphin!' presently,
And then do execution on the watch.
                 Alarum. [*They enter the town.*]

   An Alarum. [*Enter*] *Talbot in an Excursion.*

   Tal. France, thou shalt rue this treason with thy
      tears,   36
If Talbot but survive thy treachery.
Pucelle, that witch, that damned sorceress,
Hath wrought this hellish mischief unawares,
That hardly we escap'd the pride of France.   40
                      Exit.

   An Alarum: Excursions. [*Enter from the town*]
     Bedford, brought in sick in a chair. Enter
     Talbot and Burgundy, without: within, Pucelle,
     Charles, Bastard, and Alençon on the Walls.

   Joan. Good morrow, gallants! Want ye corn for
      bread?
I think the Duke of Burgundy will fast
Before he'll buy again at such a rate.
'Twas full of darnel; do you like the taste?   44
   Bur. Scoff on, vile fiend and shameless courtezan!
I trust ere long to choke thee with thine own,
And make thee curse the harvest of that corn.
   Char. Your Grace may starve perhaps, before that
      time.   48

35 S. d. Excursion: *sally against the enemy*
40 the pride of France; *cf. n.*   S. d. Alençon; *cf. n.*
44 darnel: *a weed injurious to wheat ('corn')*
46 thine own: *thy own bread*

Bed. O! let no words, but deeds, revenge this
    treason!

Joan. What will you do, good grey-beard? break
    a lance,
And run a tilt at death within a chair?

Tal. Foul fiend of France, and hag of all de-
    spite,   52
Encompass'd with thy lustful paramours!
Becomes it thee to taunt his valiant age
And twit with cowardice a man half dead?
Damsel, I'll have a bout with you again,   56
Or else let Talbot perish with this shame.

Joan. Are you so hot, sir? Yet, Pucelle, hold thy
    peace;
If Talbot do but thunder, rain will follow.

           They [i.e., Talbot, &c.,] whisper together in
                                    counsel.

God speed the parliament! who shall be the
    speaker?   60

Tal. Dare ye come forth and meet us in the field?

Joan. Belike your lordship takes us then for fools,
To try if that our own be ours or no.

Tal. I speak not to that railing Hecate,   64
But unto thee, Alençon, and the rest;
Will ye, like soldiers, come and fight it out?

Alen. Signior, no.

Tal. Signior, hang! base muleters of France! 68
Like peasant foot-boys do they keep the walls,
And dare not take up arms like gentlemen.

Joan. Away, captains! let's get us from the walls;
For Talbot means no goodness, by his looks.   72
God be wi' you, my lord! we came but to tell you

50 good grey-beard; *cf. n.*   52 of all despite: *most despicable*
64 Hecate: *goddess of witchcraft, witch*   68 muleters: *muleteers*

That we are here.

           Exeunt [Pucelle, &c.,] from the Walls.

    Tal. And there will we be too, ere it be long,

Or else reproach be Talbot's greatest fame!   76

Vow, Burgundy, by honour of thy house,—

Prick'd on by public wrongs sustain'd in France,—

Either to get the town again, or die;

And I, as sure as English Henry lives,   80

And as his father here was conqueror,

As sure as in this late-betrayed town

Great Cœur-de-lion's heart was buried,

So sure I swear to get the town or die.   84

    Bur. My vows are equal partners with thy vows

    Tal. But, ere we go, regard this dying prince,

The valiant Duke of Bedford. Come, my lord,

We will bestow you in some better place,   88

Fitter for sickness and for crazy age.

    Bed. Lord Talbot, do not so dishonour me:

Here will I sit before the walls of Roan,

And will be partner of your weal or woe.   92

    Bur. Courageous Bedford, let us now persuade
you.

    Bed. Not to be gone from hence; for once I read,

That stout Pendragon in his litter, sick,

Came to the field and vanquished his foes: 96

Methinks I should revive the soldiers' hearts,

Because I ever found them as myself.

    Tal. Undaunted spirit in a dying breast!

Then be it so: heavens keep old Bedford safe!

And now no more ado, brave Burgundy,   101

But gather we our forces out of hand,

And set upon our boasting enemy.

           Exit [with Burgundy]

81 *Cf. n.*   82, 83 *Cf. n.*   89 crazy: *broken*
95, 96 *Cf. n.*   102 out of hand: *immediately*

*An Alarum.   Excursions.   Enter Sir John Fastolfe
and a Captain.*

 Cap. Whither away, Sir John Fastolfe, in such
  haste?   104
 Fast. Whither away! to save myself by flight:
We are like to have the overthrow again.
 Cap. What! will you fly, and leave Lord Talbot?
 Fast.   Ay,
All the Talbots in the world, to save my life. 108
            Exit.
 Cap. Cowardly knight! ill fortune follow thee!
            Exit.

*Retreat.   Excursions.   Pucelle, Alençon, and
Charles fly.*

 Bed. Now, quiet soul, depart when Heaven please,
For I have seen our enemies' overthrow.
What is the trust or strength of foolish man? 112
They, that of late were daring with their scoffs,
Are glad and fain by flight to save themselves.
 Bedford dies, and is carried in by two in his chair.

An Alarum.   Enter Talbot, Burgundy, and the rest.

 Tal. Lost, and recover'd in a day again!
This is a double honour, Burgundy: 116
Yet heavens have glory for this victory!
 Bur. Warlike and martial Talbot, Burgundy
Enshrines thee in his heart, and there erects
Thy noble deeds as valour's monument.   120
 Tal. Thanks, gentle duke. But where is Pucelle
  now?
I think her old familiar is asleep.

122 familiar: *attendant demo*

Now where's the Bastard's braves, and Charles his
    gleeks?
What! all amort?   Roan hangs her head for
    grief,   124
That such a valiant company are fled.
Now will we take some order in the town,
Placing therein some expert officers,
And then depart to Paris to the king;   128
For there young Henry with his nobles lie.
    Bur. What wills Lord Talbot pleaseth Burgundy.
    Tal. But yet, before we go, let's not forget
The noble Duke of Bedford late deceas'd,   132
But see his exequies fulfill'd in Roan:
A braver soldier never couched lance,
A gentler heart did never sway in court;
But kings and mightiest potentates must die,   136
For that's the end of human misery.   *Exeunt.*

Scene Three

[Between Rouen and Paris]

*Enter Charles, Bastard, Alençon, Pucelle [and
Forces].*

    Joan. Dismay not, princes, at this accident,
Nor grieve that Roan is so recovered:
Care is no cure, but rather corrosive,
For things that are not to be remedied.   4
Let frantic Talbot triumph for a while,
And like a peacock sweep along his tail;
We'll pull his plumes and take away his train,

123 braves: *bravado*   gleeks: *gibes*
124 all amort: *'à la mort,' sick to death, prostrated*
126 some order: *certain measures*   133 exequies: *obsequies*
1 **Dismay:** *lose courage*   3 corrosive: *caustic, painful*

If Dauphin and the rest will be but rul'd.   8
   Char. We have been guided by thee hitherto,
And of thy cunning had no diffidence:
One sudden foil shall never breed distrust.
   Bast. Search out thy wit for secret policies,   12
And we will make thee famous through the world.
   Alen. We'll set thy statue in some holy place
And have thee reverenc'd like a blessed saint:
Employ thee, then, sweet virgin, for our good.   16
   Joan. Then thus it must be; this doth Joan devise:
By fair persuasions, mix'd with sugar'd words,
We will entice the Duke of Burgundy
To leave the Talbot and to follow us.   20
   Char. Ay, marry, sweeting, if we could do that,
France were no place for Henry's warriors;
Nor should that nation boast it so with us,
But be extirped from our provinces.   24
   Alen. For ever should they be expuls'd from
      France,
And not have title of an earldom here.
   Joan. Your honours shall perceive how I will work
To bring this matter to the wished end.   28
               Drum sounds afar off.
Hark! by the sound of drum you may perceive
Their powers are marching unto Paris-ward.

Here sound an English march. [*Enter, and pass
    over, Talbot and his Forces.*]

There goes the Talbot, with his colours spread,
And all the troops of English after him.   32

French march. [*Enter the Duke of Burgundy and
    his Forces.*]

Now in the rearward comes the duke and his:

10 diffidence: *distrust*   16 Employ thee: *exert thyself*
19, 20 *Cf. n.*   24 extirped: *rooted out*

Fortune in favour makes him lag behind.
Summon a parley; we will talk with him.
                              Trumpets sound a parley.
  Char. A parley with the Duke of Burgundy!
  Bur. Who craves a parley with the Burgundy? 37
  Joan. The princely Charles of France, thy country-
man.
  Bur. What sayst thou, Charles? for I am marching
hence.
  Char. Speak, Pucelle, and enchant him with thy
    words. 40
  Joan. Brave Burgundy, undoubted hope of France!
Stay, let thy humble handmaid speak to thee.
  Bur. Speak on; but be not over-tedious.
  Joan. Look on thy country, look on fertile
    France, 44
And see the cities and the towns defac'd
By wasting ruin of the cruel foe.
As looks the mother on her lowly babe
When death doth close his tender dying eyes, 48
See, see the pining malady of France;
Behold the wounds, the most unnatural wounds,
Which thou thyself hast giv'n her woeful breast.
O! turn thy edged sword another way; 52
Strike those that hurt, and hurt not those that help.
One drop of blood drawn from thy country's bosom
Should grieve thee more than streams of foreign gore:
Return thee therefore, with a flood of tears, 56
And wash away thy country's stained spots.
  Bur. Either she hath bewitch'd me with her words,
Or nature makes me suddenly relent.
  Joan. Besides, all French and France exclaims on
    thee, 60

47 lowly: *lying low* (?)

Doubting thy birth and lawful progeny.
Who join'st thou with but with a lordly nation
That will not trust thee but for profit's sake?
When Talbot hath set footing once in France,   64
And fashion'd thee that instrument of ill,
Who then but English Henry will be lord,
And thou be thrust out like a fugitive?
Call we to mind, and mark but this for proof,   68
Was not the Duke of Orleans thy foe,
And was he not in England prisoner?
But when they heard he was thine enemy,
They set him free, without his ransom paid,   72
In spite of Burgundy and all his friends.
See then, thou fight'st against thy countrymen!
And join'st with them will be thy slaughtermen.
Come, come, return; return, thou wandering lord;   76
Charles and the rest will take thee in their arms.

    Bur. I am vanquished; these haughty words of
      hers
Have batter'd me like roaring cannon-shot,
And made me almost yield upon my knees.   80
Forgive me, country, and sweet countrymen!
And, lords, accept this hearty kind embrace:
My forces and my power of men are yours.
So, farewell, Talbot; I'll no longer trust thee.   84

    Joan. Done like a Frenchman: turn, and turn
      again!
    Char. Welcome, brave duke! thy friendship makes
      us fresh.
    Bast. And doth beget new courage in our breasts.
    Alen. Pucelle hath bravely play'd her part in
      this,   88

61 progeny: *descent*   65 that instrument of: *instrument of that* (?)
69-73 *Cf. n.*   85 *Cf. n.*

And doth deserve a coronet of gold.
 Char. Now let us on, my lords, and join oui
  powers:
And seek how we may prejudice the foe.   *Exeunt.*

Scene Four

[*Paris. A Room in the Palace*]

Enter the King, Gloucester, Winchester, York, Suf-
 folk, Somerset, Warwick, Exeter [Vernon, Bas-
 set, and Others]. To them, with his Soldiers,
 Talbot.

 Tal. My gracious prince, and honourable peers,
Hearing of your arrival in this realm,
I have a while giv'n truce unto my wars,
To do my duty to my sovereign: 4
In sign whereof, this arm,—that hath reclaim'd
To your obedience fifty fortresses,
Twelve cities, and seven walled towns of strength,
Beside five hundred prisoners of esteem,—   8
Lets fall his sword before your highness' feet,
And with submissive loyalty of heart,
Ascribes the glory of his conquest got,
First to my God, and next unto your Grace.   12
 King. Is this the Lord Talbot, uncle Gloucester,
That hath so long been resident in France?
 Glo. Yes, if it please your majesty, my liege.
 King. Welcome, brave captain and victorious
  lord!   16
When I was young,—as yet I am not old,—
I do remember how my father said,
A stouter champion never handled sword.

91 prejudice: *injure*   18 *Cf.* ѕ.

Long since we were resolved of your truth,   20
Your faithful service and your toil in war;
Yet never have you tasted our reward,
Or been reguerdon'd with so much as thanks,
Because till now we never saw your face: 24
Therefore, stand up; and for these good deserts,
We here create you Earl of Shrewsbury;
And in our coronation take your place.

          Sennet. Flourish. Exeunt.

          Mane[n]t Vernon and Basset.

Ver. Now, sir, to you, that were so hot at sea,
Disgracing of these colours that I wear   29
In honour of my noble Lord of York,
Dar'st thou maintain the former words thou spak'st?
Bas. Yes, sir: as well as you dare patronage
The envious barking of your saucy tongue   33
Against my lord the Duke of Somerset.
Ver. Sirrah, thy lord I honour as he is.
Bas. Why, what is he? as good a man as York.   36
Ver. Hark ye; not so: in witness, take ye that.

          Strikes him.

Bas. Villain, thou know'st the law of arms is such
That, whoso draws a sword, 'tis present death,
Or else this blow should broach thy dearest blood.   40
But I'll unto his majesty, and crave
I may have liberty to venge this wrong;
When thou shalt see I'll meet thee to thy cost.
Ver. Well, miscreant, I'll be there as soon as
          you;   44
And, after, meet you sooner than you would.

          Exeunt.

20 resolved: *convinced*   26 *Cf. n.*   38, 39 *Cf. n.*

ACT FOURTH

Scene One

[Paris.   A Room of State]

Enter King, Gloucester, Winchester, York, Suffolk, Somerset, Warwick, Talbot, Exeter, and Governor.

Glo. Lord bishop, set the crown upon his head.
Win. God save King Henry, of that name the sixth.
Glo. Now, Governor of Paris, take your oath,—
                    [Governor kneels.]
That you elect no other king but him,   4
Esteem none friends but such as are his friends,
And none your foes but such as shall pretend
Malicious practices against his state:
This shall ye do, so help you righteous God!   8
          [The Governor takes the oath and exit.]

Enter Fastolfe.

Fast. My gracious sovereign, as I rode from Calais,
To haste unto your coronation,
A letter was deliver'd to my hands,
Writ to your Grace from the Duke of Burgundy.   12
   Tal. Shame to the Duke of Burgundy and thee!
I vow'd, base knight, when I did meet thee next,
To tear the garter from thy craven's leg;
                    [Plucking it off.]
Which I have done, because unworthily   16
Thou wast installed in that high degree.
Pardon me, princely Henry, and the rest:
This dastard, at the battle of Patay,

Act Fourth, Scene One; *cf. n.*
4 elect: *accept*   6 pretend: *purpose*
15 the garter: *Order of the Garter*   19 Patay; *cf. n.*

When but in all I was six thousand strong,   20
And that the French were almost ten to one,
Before we met or that a stroke was given,
Like to a trusty squire did run away:
In which assault we lost twelve hundred men;   24
Myself, and divers gentlemen beside,
Were there surpris'd and taken prisoners.
Then judge, great lords, if I have done amiss;
Or whether that such cowards ought to wear   28
This ornament of knighthood, yea, or no?
    Glo. To say the truth, this fact was infamous
And ill beseeming any common man,
Much more a knight, a captain and a leader.   32
    Tal. When first this order was ordain'd, my lords,
Knights of the garter were of noble birth,
Valiant and virtuous, full of haughty courage,
Such as were grown to credit by the wars;   36
Not fearing death, nor shrinking for distress,
But always resolute in most extremes.
He then that is not furnish'd in this sort
Doth but usurp the sacred name of knight,   40
Profaning this most honourable order;
And should—if I were worthy to be judge—
Be quite degraded, like a hedge-born swain
That doth presume to boast of gentle blood.   44
    King. Stain to thy countrymen! thou hear'st thy
        doom.
Be packing therefore, thou that wast a knight;
Henceforth we banish thee on pain of death.
                                [Exit Fastolfe.]
And now, my Lord Protector, view the letter   48
Sent from our uncle Duke of Burgundy.

30 fact: *misdeed*   37 distress: *physical suffering*
38 most extremes: *greatest extremities*
39 furnish'd in this sort: *so endowed*

Glo. [*Viewing superscription.*] What means his
    Grace, that he hath chang'd his style?
No more, but plain and bluntly, 'To the King!'
Hath he forgot he is his sovereign?   52
Or doth this churlish superscription
Pretend some alteration in good will?
What's here? 'I have, upon especial cause,
Mov'd with compassion of my country's wrack,
Together with the pitiful complaints   57
Of such as your oppression feeds upon,
Forsaken your pernicious faction,
And join'd with Charles, the rightful King of
    France.'   60
O, monstrous treachery! Can this be so,
That in alliance, amity, and oaths,
There should be found such false dissembling guile?
    King. What! doth my uncle Burgundy revolt?   64
    Glo. He doth, my lord, and is become your foe.
    King. Is that the worst this letter doth contain?
    Glo. It is the worst, and all, my lord, he writes.
    King. Why then, Lord Talbot there shall talk with
    him,   68
And give him chastisement for this abuse.
How say you, my lord? are you not content?
    Tal. Content, my liege! Yes: but that I am pre-
    vented,
I should have begg'd I might have been employ'd.   72
    King. Then gather strength, and march unto him
    straight:
Let him perceive how ill we brook his treason,
And what offence it is to flout his friends.
    Tal. I go, my lord; in heart desiring still   76

50 style: *mode of address*   54 Pretend: *portend*
71 prevented: *anticipated*

You may behold confusion of your foes.   [*Exit.*]

Enter Vernon and Basset.

Ver. Grant me the combat, gracious sovereign!

Bas. And me, my lord; grant me the combat too!

York. This is my servant: hear him, noble
  prince!   80

Som. And this is mine: sweet Henry, favour him!

King. Be patient, lords; and give them leave to
  speak.

Say, gentlemen, what makes you thus exclaim?

And wherefore crave you combat? or with whom? 84

Ver. With him, my lord; for he hath done me
  wrong.

Bas. And I with him; for he hath done me wrong.

King. What is that wrong whereof you both com-
  plain?

First let me know, and then I'll answer you.   88

Bas. Crossing the sea from England into France,

This fellow here, with envious carping tongue,

Upbraided me about the rose I wear;

Saying, the sanguine colour of the leaves   92

Did represent my master's blushing cheeks,

When stubbornly he did repugn the truth

About a certain question in the law

Argu'd betwixt the Duke of York and him;   96

With other vile and ignominious terms:

In confutation of which rude reproach,

And in defence of my lord's worthiness,

I crave the benefit of law of arms.   100

Ver. And that is my petition, noble lord:

For though he seem with forged quaint conceit,

To set a gloss upon his bold intent,

78 the combat: *license to fight*   94 repugn: *repudiate*
102 quaint: *ingenious*

Yet know, my lord, I was provok'd by him;   104
And he first took exceptions at this badge,
Pronouncing that the paleness of this flower
Bewray'd the faintness of my master's heart.

York. Will not this malice, Somerset, be left?   108

Som. Your private grudge, my Lord of York, will
   out,
Though ne'er so cunningly you smother it.

King. Good Lord! what madness rules in brain-
   sick men,
When, for so slight and frivolous a cause,   112
Such factious emulations shall arise!
Good cousins both, of York and Somerset,
Quiet yourselves, I pray, and be at peace.

York. Let this dissension first be tried by
   fight,   116
And then your highness shall command a peace.

Som. The quarrel toucheth none but us alone;
Betwixt ourselves let us decide it, then.

York. There is my pledge; accept it, Somerset.   120

Ver. Nay, let it rest where it began at first.

Bas. Confirm it so, mine honourable lord.

Glo. Confirm it so! Confounded be your strife!
And perish ye, with your audacious prate!   124
Presumptuous vassals! are you not asham'd,
With this immodest clamorous outrage
To trouble and disturb the king and us?—
And you, my lords, methinks you do not well   128
To bear with their perverse objections;
Much less to take occasion from their mouths
To raise a mutiny betwixt yourselves:
Let me persuade you take a better course.   132

124 prate: *prating*   126 immodest: *immoderate, presumptuous*
129 objections: *accusations*

Exe. It grieves his highness: good my lords, be
    friends.
King. Come hither, you that would be combatants.
Henceforth I charge you, as you love our favour,
Quite to forget this quarrel and the cause.   136
And you, my lords, remember where we are;
In France, amongst a fickle wavering nation.
If they perceive dissension in our looks,
And that within ourselves we disagree,   140
How will their grudging stomachs be provok'd
To wilful disobedience, and rebel!
Beside, what infamy will there arise,
When foreign princes shall be certified   144
That for a toy, a thing of no regard,
King Henry's peers and chief nobility
Destroy'd themselves, and lost the realm of France!
O! think upon the conquest of my father,   148
My tender years, and let us not forgo
That for a trifle that was bought with blood!
Let me be umpire in this doubtful strife.
I see no reason, if I wear this rose,   152
                        [*Putting on a red rose.*]
That any one should therefore be suspicious
I more incline to Somerset than York:
Both are my kinsmen, and I love them both.
As well they may upbraid me with my crown,   156
Because, forsooth, the King of Scots is crown'd.
But your discretions better can persuade
Than I am able to instruct or teach:
And therefore, as we hither came in peace,   160
So let us still continue peace and love.
Cousin of York, we institute your Grace

140 within: *among*   141 grudging stomachs: *rebellious tempers*
145 toy: *whim, trifle*

To be our regent in these parts of France:
And, good my Lord of Somerset, unite   164
Your troops of horsemen with his bands of foot;
And like true subjects, sons of your progenitors,
Go cheerfully together and digest
Your angry choler on your enemies.   168
Ourself, my Lord Protector, and the rest,
After some respite will return to Calais;
From thence to England; where I hope ere long
To be presented by your victories,   172
With Charles, Alençon, and that traitorous rout.
            Exeunt. Mane[n]t York, Warwick, Exeter,
                                    Vernon.
    War. My Lord of York, I promise you, the king
Prettily, methought, did play the orator.
    York. And so he did; but yet I like it not,
In that he wears the badge of Somerset.   177
    War. Tush! that was but his fancy, blame him not;
I dare presume, sweet prince, he thought no harm.
    York. An if I wist he did,—But let it rest;
Other affairs must now be managed.   181
                    Exeunt. Flourish. Manet Exeter.
    Exe. Well didst thou, Richard, to suppress thy
            voice;
For had the passions of thy heart burst out,
I fear we should have seen decipher'd there   184
More rancorous spite, more furious raging broils,
Than yet can be imagin'd or suppos'd.
But howsoe'er, no simple man that sees
This jarring discord of nobility,   188
This shouldering of each other in the court,
This factious bandying of their favourites,

---

167 digest: *vent, disperse*   181 S. d. Flourish; *cf. n.*
190 bandying: *contending*

But that it doth presage some ill event.   191
'Tis much when sceptres are in children's hands;
But more, when envy breeds unkind division:
There comes the ruin, there begins confusion.   *Exit.*

Scene Two

[*Before Bordeaux*]

Enter Talbot, with Trump and Drum, before Bordeaux.

Tal. Go to the gates of Bordeaux, trumpeter;
Summon their general unto the wall.

[Trumpet] sounds. Enter General aloft [with followers].

English John Talbot, captains, calls you forth.
Servant in arms to Harry King of England;   4
And thus he would: Open your city gates,
Be humble to us, call my sovereign yours,
And do him homage as obedient subjects,
And I'll withdraw me and my bloody power;   8
But, if you frown upon this proffer'd peace,
You tempt the fury of my three attendants,
Lean famine, quartering steel, and climbing fire;
Who in a moment even with the earth   12
Shall lay your stately and air-braving towers,
If you forsake the offer of their love.
   Gen. Thou ominous and fearful owl of death,
Our nation's terror and their bloody scourge!   16
The period of thy tyranny approacheth.
On us thou canst not enter but by death;

191 But: *but sees, i.e., without seeing*   193 unkind: *unnatural*
Scene Two; *cf. n.*   5 would: *would have you understand*
10, 11 *Cf. n.*   17 period: *full stop, end*

For, I protest, we are well fortified,
And strong enough to issue out and fight: 20
If thou retire, the Dauphin, well appointed,
Stands with the snares of war to tangle thee:
On either hand thee there are squadrons pitch'd,
To wall thee from the liberty of flight;   24
And no way canst thou turn thee for redress
But death doth front thee with apparent spoil,
And pale destruction meets thee in the face.
Ten thousand French have ta'en the sacrament,   28
To rive their dangerous artillery
Upon no Christian soul but English Talbot.
Lo! there thou stand'st, a breathing valiant man,
Of an invincible unconquer'd spirit: 32
This is the latest glory of thy praise,
That I, thy enemy, 'due thee withal;
For ere the glass, that now begins to run,
Finish the process of his sandy hour,   36
These eyes, that see thee now well coloured,
Shall see thee wither'd, bloody, pale, and dead.
                  Drum afar off.
Hark! hark! the Dauphin's drum, a warning bell,
Sings heavy music to thy timorous soul;   40
And mine shall ring thy dire departure out.   *Exit.*
   Tal. He fables not; I hear the enemy:
Out, some light horsemen, and peruse their wings.
O! negligent and heedless discipline;   44
How are we park'd and bounded in a pale,
A little herd of England's timorous deer,
Maz'd with a yelping kennel of French curs!
If we be English deer, be, then, in blood;   48

23 either hand: *both sides of*   25 redress: *aid*
26 apparent spoil: *obvious ruin*   29 rive: *cause to burst, discharge*
43 peruse their wings: *reconnoitre their flanks*
44 discipline: *tactics*   45 park'd: *enclosed*   pale: *fence*
47 Maz'd: *bewildered*   48 in blood: *vigorous*

Not rascal-like, to fall down with a pinch,
But rather, moody-mad and desperate stags,
Turn on the bloody hounds with heads of steel,
And make the cowards stand aloof at bay: 52
Sell every man his life as dear as mine,
And they shall find dear deer of us, my friends.
God and Saint George, Talbot and England's right,
Prosper our colours in this dangerous fight!   56

[Exeunt.]

Scene Three

[Plains in Gascony]

*Enter a Messenger that meets York.   Enter York
with Trumpet and many Soldiers.*

York. Are not the speedy scouts return'd again,
That dogg'd the mighty army of the Dauphin?
Mess. They are return'd, my lord; and give it out,
That he is march'd to Bordeaux with his power,
To fight with Talbot. As he march'd along,   5
By your espials were discovered
Two mightier troops than that the Dauphin led,
Which join'd with him and made their march for
    Bordeaux.   8
York. A plague upon that villain Somerset,
That thus delays my promised supply
Of horsemen that were levied for this siege!
Renowned Talbot doth expect my aid,   12
And I am louted by a traitor villain,
And cannot help the noble chevalier.
God comfort him in this necessity!
If he miscarry, farewell wars in France.   16

49 rascal-like: *like a lean and jaded deer*   13 louted: *mocked*

Enter another Messenger [Sir William Lucy].

Sec. Mess. Thou princely leader of our English
  strength,
Never so needful on the earth of France,
Spur to the rescue of the noble Talbot,
Who now is girdled with a waist of iron   **20**
And hemm'd about with grim destruction.
To Bordeaux, warlike duke! To Bordeaux, York!
Else, farewell Talbot, France, and England's honour.
  York. O God! that Somerset, who in proud
    heart   **24**
Doth stop my cornets, were in Talbot's place!
So should we save a valiant gentleman
By forfeiting a traitor and a coward.
Mad ire and wrathful fury makes me weep   **28**
That thus we die, while remiss traitors sleep.
  Sec. Mess. O! send some succour to the distress'd
    lord.
  York. He dies, we lose; I break my warlike word;
We mourn, France smiles; we lose, they daily get;   **32**
All long of this vile traitor Somerset.
  Sec. Mess. Then God take mercy on brave Talbot's
    soul;
And on his son young John, whom two hours since
I met in travel toward his warlike father.   **36**
This seven years did not Talbot see his son;
And now they meet where both their lives are done.
  York. Alas! what joy shall noble Talbot have
To bid his young son welcome to his grave?   **40**
Away! vexation almost stops my breath
That sunder'd friends greet in the hour of death.
Lucy, farewell: no more my fortune can,
But curse the cause I cannot aid the man.   **44**

25 cornets: *troops of horse*   33 long of: *on account of*

Maine, Blois, Poitiers, and Tours, are won away,
Long all of Somerset and his delay.

                                     Exit [*with his Soldiers*].

   Sec. Mess. Thus, while the vulture of sedition
Feeds in the bosom of such great commanders,   48
Sleeping neglection doth betray to loss
The conquest of our scarce cold conqueror,
That ever living man of memory,
Henry the Fifth. Whiles they each other cross,
Lives, honours, lands. and all hurry to loss.   53

Scene Four

[*The Same*]

Enter Somerset, with his Army [*and a Captain of
Talbot's*].

   Som. It is too late; I cannot send them now:
This expedition was by York and Talbot
Too rashly plotted: all our general force
Might with a sally of the very town   4
Be buckled with: the over-daring Talbot
Hath sullied all his gloss of former honour
By this unheedful, desperate, wild adventure:
York set him on to fight and die in shame,   8
That, Talbot dead, great York might bear the name.
   Cap. Here is Sir William Lucy, who with me
Set from our o'ermatch'd forces forth for aid.
   Som. How now, Sir William! whither were you
     sent?   12

47 vulture of sedition; *cf. n.*
49 Sleeping neglection: *slothful neglect*
50 scarce cold conqueror; *cf. n.*
Scene Four; *cf. n.*
4 the very town: *the mere garrison* (*unsupported by the relieving
armies*)

Lucy. Whither, my lord? from bought and sold
   Lord Talbot;
Who, ring'd about with bold adversity,
Cries out for noble York and Somerset,
To beat assailing death from his weak legions: 16
And whiles the honourable captain there
Drops bloody sweat from his war-wearied limbs,
And, in advantage lingering, looks for rescue,
You, his false hopes, the trust of England's
   honour,   20
Keep off aloof with worthless emulation.
Let not your private discord keep away
The levied succours that should lend him aid,
While he, renowned noble gentleman,   24
Yields up his life unto a world of odds:
Orleans the Bastard, Charles, Burgundy,
Alençon, Reignier, compass him about,
And Talbot perisheth by your default.   28
   Som. York set him on; York should have sent him
   aid.
   Lucy. And York as fast upon your Grace exclaims;
Swearing that you withhold his levied host
Collected for this expedition.   32
   Som. York lies; he might have sent and had the
   horse:
I owe him little duty, and less love;
And take foul scorn to fawn on him by sending.
   Lucy. The fraud of England, not the force of
   France,   36
Hath now entrapp'd the noble-minded Talbot.
Never to England shall he bear his life,
But dies, betray'd to fortune by your strife.

13 Whither, my lord; *cf. n.*
19 in advantage lingering: *making the most of every desperate
chance (?)*   21 worthless: *unworthy*

Som. Come, go; I will dispatch the horsemen
  straight: 40
Within six hours they will be at his aid.
  Lucy. Too late comes rescue: he is ta'en or slain,
For fly he could not if he would have fled;
And fly would Talbot never, though he might.   44
  Som. If he be dead, brave Talbot, then adieu!
  Lucy. His fame lives in the world, his shame in
  you.   *Exeunt.*

Scene Five

[*Castillon, near Bordeaux*]

Enter Talbot and his Son.

  Tal. O young John Talbot! I did send for thee
To tutor thee in stratagems of war,
That Talbot's name might be in thee reviv'd
When sapless age, and weak unable limbs   4
Should bring thy father to his drooping chair.
But,—O malignant and ill-boding stars!
Now thou art come unto a feast of death,
A terrible and unavoided danger: 8
Therefore, dear boy, mount on my swiftest horse,
And I'll direct thee how thou shalt escape
By sudden flight: come, dally not, be gone.
  John. Is my name Talbot? and am I your son?   12
And shall I fly? O! if you love my mother,
Dishonour not her honourable name,
To make a bastard and a slave of me:
The world will say he is not Talbot's blood   16
That basely fled when noble Talbot stood.
  Tal. Fly, to revenge my death, if I be slain.

8 unavoided: *unavoidable*

John. He that flies so will ne'er return again.

Tal. If we both stay, we both are sure to die.   20

John. Then let me stay; and, father, do you fly:
Your loss is great, so your regard should be;
My worth unknown, no loss is known in me.
Upon my death the French can little boast;   24
In yours they will, in you all hopes are lost.
Flight cannot stain the honour you have won;
But mine it will that no exploit have done:
You fled for vantage everyone will swear;   28
But if I bow, they'll say it was for fear.
There is no hope that ever I will stay
If the first hour I shrink and run away.
Here, on my knee, I beg mortality,   32
Rather than life preserv'd with infamy.

Tal. Shall all thy mother's hopes lie in one tomb?

John. Ay, rather than I'll shame my mother's womb.

Tal. Upon my blessing I command thee go.   36

John. To fight I will, but not to fly the foe.

Tal. Part of thy father may be sav'd in thee.

John. No part of him but will be shame in me.

Tal. Thou never hadst renown, nor canst not lose it.   40

John. Yes, your renowned name: shall flight abuse it?

Tal. Thy father's charge shall clear thee from that stain.

John. You cannot witness for me, being slain.
If death be so apparent, then both fly.   44

Tal. And leave my followers here to fight and die?
My age was never tainted with such shame.

John. And shall my youth be guilty of such blame?

22 regard: *care (of yourself:*

No more can I be sever'd from your side   48
Than can yourself yourself in twain divide.
Stay, go, do what you will, the like do I;
For live I will not if my father die.

  Tal. Then here I take my leave of thee, fair
      son,   52
Born to eclipse thy life this afternoon.
Come, side by side together live and die,
And soul with soul from France to heaven fly.

                                    Exeunt.

                    Scene Six

                   [*The Same*]

*Alarum: Excursions, wherein Talbot's Son is hemmed
        about, and Talbot rescues him.*

  Tal. Saint George and victory! fight, soldiers,
      fight!
The regent hath with Talbot broke his word,
And left us to the rage of France his sword.
Where is John Talbot? Pause, and take thy
      breath: 4
I gave thee life and rescu'd thee from death.

  John. O! twice my father, twice am I thy son:
The life thou gav'st me first was lost and done,
Till with thy warlike sword, despite of fate,   8
To my determin'd time thou gav'st new date.

  Tal. When from the Dauphin's crest thy sword
      struck fire,
It warm'd thy father's heart with proud desire
Of bold-fac'd victory. Then leaden age,   12
Quicken'd with youthful spleen and warlike rage,

3 France his: *France's*   9 determin'd: *ended*

Beat down Alençon, Orleans, Burgundy,
And from the pride of Gallia rescu'd thee.
The ireful bastard Orleans,—that drew blood   16
From thee, my boy, and had the maidenhood
Of thy first fight,—I soon encountered
And, interchanging blows, I quickly shed
Some of his bastard blood; and, in disgrace,   20
Bespoke him thus, 'Contaminated, base,
And misbegotten blood I spill of thine,
Mean and right poor, for that pure blood of mine
Which thou didst force from Talbot, my brave
    boy.'   24
Here, purposing the Bastard to destroy,
Came in strong rescue. Speak, thy father's care,
Art thou not weary, John? How dost thou fare?
Wilt thou yet leave the battle, boy, and fly,   28
Now thou art seal'd the son of chivalry?
Fly, to revenge my death when I am dead;
The help of one stands me in little stead.
O! too much folly is it, well I wot,   32
To hazard all our lives in one small boat.
If I to-day die not with Frenchmen's rage,
To-morrow I shall die with mickle age:
By me they nothing gain an if I stay;   36
'Tis but the short'ning of my life one day.
In thee thy mother dies, our household's name,
My death's revenge, thy youth, and England's fame.
All these and more we hazard by thy stay;   40
All these are sav'd if thou wilt fly away.
    John. The sword of Orleans hath not made me
        smart;
These words of yours draw life-blood from my heart.
On that advantage, bought with such a shame,   44

25 purposing: *as I purposed*   44 On that advantage; *cf. n.*

To save a paltry life and slay bright fame,
Before young Talbot from old Talbot fly,
The coward horse that bears me fall and die!
And like me to the peasant boys of France,   48
To be shame's scorn and subject of mischance!
Surely, by all the glory you have won,
An if I fly, I am not Talbot's son:
Then talk no more of flight, it is no boot;   52
If son to Talbot, die at Talbot's foot.

    Tal. Then follow thou thy desperate sire of Crete,
Thou Icarus. Thy life to me is sweet:
If thou wilt fight, fight by thy father's side,   56
And, commendable prov'd, let's die in pride.

                                        Exeunt.

Scene Seven

[*The Same*]

*Alarum: Excursions. Enter Old Talbot, led [by a
Servant].*

    Tal. Where is my other life?—mine own is gone;—
O! where's young Talbot? where is valiant John?
Triumphant death, smear'd with captivity,
Young Talbot's valour makes me smile at thee.   4
When he perceiv'd me shrink and on my knee,
His bloody sword he brandish'd over me,
And like a hungry lion did commence
Rough deeds of rage and stern impatience;   8
But when my angry guardant stood alone,
Tendering my ruin and assail'd of none,
Dizzy-ey'd fury and great rage of heart

---

48 like: *liken*   54 sire of Crete: *i.e., Dædalus*
3 smear'd with captivity: *thyself besmirched with defeat*
9 guardant: *guardian*   10 Tendering: *solicitous over*

Suddenly made him from my side to start   12
Into the clust'ring battle of the French;
And in that sea of blood my boy did drench
His overmounting spirit; and there died
My Icarus, my blossom, in his pride.   16

 Enter [Soldiers] with John Talbot, borne.

 Serv. O, my dear lord! lo, where your son is borne!
 Tal. Thou antic, death, which laugh'st us here to
  scorn,
Anon, from thy insulting tyranny,
Coupled in bonds of perpetuity,   20
Two Talbots, winged through the lither sky,
In thy despite shall 'scape mortality.
O! thou, whose wounds become hard-favour'd death,
Speak to thy father ere thou yield thy breath;   24
Brave death by speaking whether he will or no;
Imagine him a Frenchman and thy foe.
Poor boy! he smiles, methinks, as who should say,
Had death been French, then death had died
  to-day.   28
Come, come, and lay him in his father's arms:
My spirit can no longer bear these harms.
Soldiers, adieu! I have what I would have,
Now my old arms are young John Talbot's grave.   32
          Dies.

 Enter Charles, Alençon, Burgundy, Bastard and
      Pucelle.

 Char. Had York and Somerset brought rescue in,
We should have found a bloody day of this.
 Bast. How the young whelp of Talbot's, raging-
  wood,

13 battle: *main body*   18 antic: *buffoon*
21 lither: *yielding*   23 become hard-favour'd: *beautify ugly*
25 Brave: *defy*   35 raging-wood: *mad with rage*

Did flesh his puny sword in Frenchmen's blood!   36

   Joan. Once I encounter'd him, and thus I said:
'Thou maiden youth, be vanquish'd by a maid':
But with a proud majestical high scorn,
He answer'd thus: 'Young Talbot was not born   40
To be the pillage of a giglot wench.'
So, rushing in the bowels of the French,
He left me proudly, as unworthy fight.

   Bur. Doubtless he would have made a noble
     knight;   44
See, where he lies inhearsed in the arms
Of the most bloody nurser of his harms.

   Bast. Hew them to pieces, hack their bones asunder,
Whose life was England's glory, Gallia's wonder.

   Char. O, no! forbear; for that which we have
     fled   49
During the life, let us not wrong it dead.

     Enter Lucy [with a French Herald].

   Lucy. Herald, conduct me to the Dauphin's tent,
To know who hath obtain'd the glory of the day.

   Char. On what submissive message art thou
     sent?   53

   Lucy. Submission, Dauphin! 'tis a mere French
     word;
We English warriors wot not what it means.
I come to know what prisoners thou hast ta'en,   56
And to survey the bodies of the dead.

   Char. For prisoners ask'st thou? hell our prison is.
But tell me whom thou seek'st.

   Lucy. Where is the great Alcides of the field,   60
Valiant Lord Talbot, Earl of Shrewsbury?
Created, for his rare success in arms,

---

41 giglot: *wanton*   44 Doubtless: *undoubtedly*

Great Earl of Washford, Waterford, and Valence;
Lord Talbot of Goodrig and Urchinfield,   64
Lord Strange of Blackmere, Lord Verdon of Alton,
Lord Cromwell of Wingfield, Lord Furnivall of Shef-
    field,
The thrice-victorious Lord of Falconbridge;
Knight of the noble order of Saint George,   68
Worthy Saint Michael and the Golden Fleece;
Great mareschal to Henry the Sixth
Of all his wars within the realm of France?
    Joan. Here is a silly stately style indeed!   72
The Turk, that two-and-fifty kingdoms hath,
Writes not so tedious a style as this.
Him that thou magnifiest with all these titles,
Stinking and fly-blown lies here at our feet.   76
    Lucy. Is Talbot slain, the Frenchmen's only
    scourge,
Your kingdom's terror and black Nemesis?
O! were mine eye-balls into bullets turn'd,
That I in rage might shoot them at your faces!   80
O! that I could but call these dead to life!
It were enough to fright the realm of France.
Were but his picture left among you here,
It would amaze the proudest of you all.   84
Give me their bodies, that I may bear them hence,
And give them burial as beseems their worth.
    Joan. I think this upstart is old Talbot's ghost,
He speaks with such a proud commanding spirit.
For God's sake, let him have 'em; to keep them
    here   89
They would but stink and putrefy the air.
    Char. Go, take their bodies hence.

63-71 *Cf. n.*   72 style: *title*
84 amaze: *astound*   89, 94 'em; *cf. n.*

Lucy.   I'll bear them hence:
But from their ashes shall be rear'd   92
A phœnix that shall make all France afeard.
    Char. So we be rid of them, do with 'em what thou
    wilt.
And now to Paris, in this conquering vein:
All will be ours now bloody Talbot's slain.   96

                                        Exeunt.

ACT FIFTH

Scene One

[*London.   A Room in the Palace*]

Sennet.   Enter King, Gloucester, and Exeter.

    King. Have you perus'd the letters from the pope,
The emperor, and the Earl of Armagnac?
    Glo. I have, my lord; and their intent is this:
They humbly sue unto your excellence   4
To have a godly peace concluded of
Between the realms of England and of France.
    King. How doth your Grace affect their motion?
    Glo. Well,   my   good   lord;   and   as   the   only
    means   8
To stop effusion of our Christian blood,
And stablish quietness on every side.
    King. Ay, marry, uncle; for I always thought
It was both impious and unnatural   12
That such immanity and bloody strife
Should reign among professors of one faith.
    Glo. Beside, my lord, the sooner to effect

1, 2 *Cf. n.*   7 affect: *incline toward*   13 immanity: *ferocity*

And surer bind this knot of amity,   16
The Earl of Armagnac, near knit to Charles,
A man of great authority in France,
Proffers his only daughter to your Grace
In marriage, with a large and sumptuous dowry.
    King. Marriage, uncle! alas! my years are
      young,   21
And fitter is my study and my books
Than wanton dalliance with a paramour.
Yet call the ambassadors; and, as you please,   24
So let them have their answers every one:
I shall be well content with any choice
Tends to God's glory and my country's weal.

*Enter Winchester [dressed as Cardinal], and three
    Ambassadors [one a Papal Legate].*

    Exe. [Aside.] What! is my Lord of Winchester
      install'd,   28
And call'd unto a cardinal's degree?
Then, I perceive that will be verified
Henry the Fifth did sometime prophesy,—
'If once he come to be a cardinal,   32
He'll make his cap co-equal with the crown.'
    King. My lords ambassadors, your several suits
Have been consider'd and debated on.
Your purpose is both good and reasonable;   36
And therefore are we certainly resolv'd
To draw conditions of a friendly peace;
Which by my Lord of Winchester we mean
Shall be transported presently to France.   40
    Glo. And for the proffer of my lord your master,
I have inform'd his highness so at large,
As,—liking of the lady's virtuous gifts,

31 sometime: *formerly*   43 As: *that*

Her beauty, and the value of her dower,—   44
He doth intend she shall be England's queen.
   King. In argument and proof of which contract,
Bear her this jewel, pledge of my affection.
And so, my lord protector, see them guarded   48
And safely brought to Dover; where inshipp'd
Commit them to the fortune of the sea.
       Exeunt [all but Winchester and the Legate].
   Win. Stay, my lord legate: you shall first receive
The sum of money which I promised   52
Should be deliver'd to his holiness
For clothing me in these grave ornaments.
   Leg. I will attend upon your lordship's leisure.
   Win. [*Aside.*] Now Winchester will not submit, I
    trow,   56
Or be inferior to the proudest peer.
Humphrey of Gloucester, thou shalt well perceive
That neither in birth or for authority
The bishop will be overborne by thee: 60
I'll either make thee stoop and bend thy knee,
Or sack this country with a mutiny.   *Exeunt.*

Scene Two

[*France.   Plains in Anjou ?*]

*Enter Charles, Burgundy, Alençon, Bastard,
Reignier, and Joan.*

   Char. These news, my lord, may cheer our droop-
    ing spirits;
'Tis said the stout Parisians do revolt,
And turn again unto the warlike French.
   Alen. Then, march to Paris, royal Charles of
    France,   4

And keep not back your powers in dalliance.
  Joan. Peace be amongst them if they turn to us;
Else, ruin combat with their palaces!

Enter Scout.

  Scout. Success unto our valiant general,   8
And happiness to his accomplices!
  Char. What tidings send our scouts? I prithee
    speak.
  Scout. The English army, that divided was
Into two parties, is now conjoin'd in one,   12
And means to give you battle presently.
  Char. Somewhat too sudden, sirs, the warning is:
But we will presently provide for them.
  Bur. I trust the ghost of Talbot is not there: 16
Now he is gone, my lord, you need not fear.
  Joan. Of all base passions, fear is most accurs'd.
Command the conquest, Charles, it shall be thine;
Let Henry fret and all the world repine.   20
  Char. Then on, my lords; and France be fortu-
    nate!

Exeunt. Alarum. Excursions.

Scene Three

[*The Same*]

Enter Joan la Pucelle.

  Joan. The regent conquers and the Frenchmen fly.
Now help, ye charming spells and periapts;
And ye choice spirits that admonish me
And give me signs of future accidents: *Thunder.*
You speedy helpers, that are substitutes   5

---

1 accomplices: *comrades*   1 The regent conquers; *cf. n.*
2 periapts: *amulets*   4 accidents: *events*   5 substitutes: *agents*

Under the lordly monarch of the north,
Appear, and aid me in this enterprise!

Enter Fiends.

This speedy and quick appearance argues proof
Of your accustom'd diligence to me. $

Now, ye familiar spirits, that are cull'd
Out of the powerful regions under earth,
Help me this once, that France may get the field.
                     They walk, and speak not.
O! hold me not with silence over-long.   13
Where I was wont to feed you with my blood,
I'll lop a member off and give it you,
In earnest of a further benefit,   14
So you do condescend to help me now.
                     They hang their heads.
No hope to have redress? My body shall
Pay recompense, if you will grant my suit.
                     They shake their heads.
Cannot my body nor blood-sacrifice   20
Entreat you to your wonted furtherance?
Then take my soul; my body, soul, and all,
Before that England give the French the foil.
                           They depart.
See! they forsake me. Now the time is come,   24
That France must vail her lofty-plumed crest,
And let her head fall into England's lap.
My ancient incantations are too weak,
And hell too strong for me to buckle with: 28
Now, France, thy glory droopeth to the dust. *Exit.*

*Excursions. Burgundy and York fight hand to hand.
   French fly [leaving Joan in York's power].*

6 monarch of the north: *cf. n.*   25 vail: *lower*
29 S. d. Burgundy and York fight; *cf. n.*

York. Damsel of France, I think I have you fast:
Unchain your spirits now with spelling charms,
And try if they can gain your liberty.   32
A goodly prize, fit for the devil's grace!
See how the ugly witch doth bend her brows,
As if with Circe she would change my shape.
   Joan. Chang'd to a worser shape thou canst not
     be.   36
   York. O! Charles the Dauphin is a proper man;
No shape but his can please your dainty eye.
   Joan. A plaguing mischief light on Charles and
     thee!
And may ye both be suddenly surpris'd   40
By bloody hands, in sleeping on your beds!
   York. Fell banning hag, enchantress, hold thy
     tongue!
   Joan. I prithee, give me leave to curse a while.
   York. Curse, miscreant, when thou comest to the
     stake.   *Exeunt.*
Alarum. Enter Suffolk, with Margaret in his hand.

   Suf. Be what thou wilt, thou art my prisoner.
                        Gazes on her.
O fairest beauty! do not fear nor fly,
For I will touch thee but with reverent hands.
I kiss these fingers for eternal peace,   48
And lay them gently on thy tender side.
What art thou? say, that I may honour thee.
   Mar. Margaret my name, and daughter to a king,
The King of Naples, whosoe'er thou art.   52
   Suf. An earl I am, and Suffolk am I call'd.
Be not offended, nature's miracle,
Thou art allotted to be ta'en by me:

31 spelling: *working spells*   35 with Circe: *Circe-like*
37 proper: *handsome*   42 Fell: *fierce*
48 for: *in token of*   55 allotted: *appointed (by fate)*

So doth the swan her downy cygnets save,   56
Keeping them prisoners underneath her wings.
Yet if this servile usage once offend,
Go and be free again, as Suffolk's friend.

                                        She is going.

O stay! I have no power to let her pass;   60
My hand would free her, but my heart says no.
As plays the sun upon the glassy streams,
Twinkling another counterfeited beam,
So seems this gorgeous beauty to mine eyes.   64
Fain would I woo her, yet I dare not speak:
I'll call for pen and ink and write my mind.
Fie, De la Pole! disable not thyself;
Hast not a tongue? is she not here?   68
Wilt thou be daunted at a woman's sight?
Ay; beauty's princely majesty is such
Confounds the tongue and makes the senses rough.

   Mar. Say, Earl of Suffolk,—if thy name be
    so,—   72
What ransom must I pay before I pass?
For I perceive, I am thy prisoner.

   Suf. [*Aside.*] How canst thou tell she will deny
    thy suit,
Before thou make a trial of her love?   76

   Mar. Why speak'st thou not? what ransom must
    I pay?

   Suf. [*Aside.*] She's beautiful and therefore to be
    woo'd,
She is a woman, therefore to be won.

   Mar. Wilt thou accept of ransom, yea or no?

   Suf. [*Aside.*] Fond man! remember that thou hast
    a wife;   81

63 *Cf. n.*   67 disable: *disparage*
68 *Cf. n.*   71 Confounds: *that it confounds*
75 S. d. Aside· *cf. n.*   78, 79 *Cf. n.*

Then how can Margaret be thy paramour?

   Mar. I were best to leave him, for he will not hear.

   Suf. [*Aside.*] There all is marr'd; there lies a cool-
     ing card.   84

   Mar. He talks at random; sure, the man is mad.

   Suf. [*Aside.*] And yet a dispensation may be had.

   Mar. And yet I would that you would answer me.

   Suf. [*Aside.*] I'll win this Lady Margaret. For
     whom?   88

Why, for my king: tush! that's a wooden thing.

   Mar. [*Overhearing him.*] He talks of wood: it is
     some carpenter.

   Suf. [*Aside.*] Yet so my fancy may be satisfied,

And peace established between these realms.   92

But there remains a scruple in that too;

For though her father be the King of Naples,

Duke of Anjou and Maine, yet is he poor,

And our nobility will scorn the match.   96

   Mar. Hear ye, captain? Are you not at leisure?

   Suf. [*Aside.*] It shall be so, disdain they ne'er so
     much:

Henry is youthful and will quickly yield.

Madam, I have a secret to reveal.   100

   Mar. [*Aside.*] What though I be enthrall'd? he
     seems a knight,

And will not any way dishonour me.

   Suf. Lady, vouchsafe to listen what I say.

   Mar. [*Aside.*] Perhaps I shall be rescu'd by the
     French;   104

And then I need not crave his courtesy.

   Suf. Sweet madam, give me hearing in a cause—

   Mar. Tush, women have been captivate ere now.

---

84 cooling card: *card (played by an adversary) which dashes one's
   hope*   91 fancy: *love*

Suf. Lady, wherefore talk you so?   108
Mar. I cry you mercy, 'tis but *quid* for *quo.*
Suf. Say, gentle princess, would you not suppose
Your bondage happy to be made a queen?
Mar. To be a queen in bondage is more vile
Than is a slave in base servility;   113
For princes should be free.
Suf.   And so shall you,
If happy England's royal king be free.
Mar. Why, what concerns his freedom unto
me?   116
Suf. I'll undertake to make thee Henry's queen,
To put a golden sceptre in thy hand
And set a precious crown upon thy head,
If thou wilt condescend to be my—
Mar.   What?
Suf.   His love.   120
Mar. I am unworthy to be Henry's wife.
Suf. No, gentle madam; I unworthy am
To woo so fair a dame to be his wife
And have no portion in the choice myself.   124
How say you, madam, are you so content?
Mar. An if my father please, I am content.
Suf. Then call our captains and our colours forth!
And, madam, at your father's castle walls   128
We'll crave a parley, to confer with him.

                 Sound.   Enter Reignier on the Walls.

Suf. See, Reignier, see thy daughter prisoner!
Reig. To whom?
Suf.   To me.
Reig.   Suffolk, what remedy?
I am a soldier, and unapt to weep,   132

111 to be: *if you were in consequence*   132 unapt: *disinclined*

Or to exclaim on Fortune's fickleness.
  Suf. Yes, there is remedy enough, my lord:
Consent, and for thy honour give consent,
Thy daughter shall be wedded to my king,   13ხ
Whom I with pain have woo'd and won thereto;
And this her easy-held imprisonment
Hath gain'd thy daughter princely liberty.
  Reig. Speaks Suffolk as he thinks?
  Suf.   Fair Margaret knows   140
That Suffolk doth not flatter, face, or feign.
  Reig. Upon thy princely warrant, I descend
To give thee answer of thy just demand.
                    [*Exit from the walls.*]
  Suf. And here I will expect thy coming.   144

        Trumpets sound. Enter Reignier [below].

  Reig. Welcome, brave earl, into our territories:
Command in Anjou what your honour pleases.
  Suf. Thanks, Reignier, happy for so sweet a child,
Fit to be made companion with a king.   148
What answer makes your Grace unto my suit?
  Reig. Since thou dost deign to woo her little worth
To be the princely bride of such a lord,
Upon condition I may quietly   152
Enjoy mine own, the country Maine and Anjou,
Free from oppression or the stroke of war,
My daughter shall be Henry's if he please.
  Suf. That is her ransom; I deliver her;   156
And those two counties I will undertake
Your Grace shall well and quietly enjoy.
  Reig. And I again, in Henry's royal name,
As deputy unto that gracious king,   160
Give thee her hand for sign of plighted faith.

141 face: *wear a false face*

Suf. Reignier of France, I give thee kingly thanks,
Because this is in traffic of a king.
[*Aside.*] And yet, methinks, I could be well con-
    tent   164
To be mine own attorney in this case.
I'll over, then, to England with this news,
And make this marriage to be solemniz'd.
So farewell, Reignier: set this diamond safe,   168
In golden palaces, as it becomes.
    Reig. I do embrace thee, as I would embrace
The Christian prince, King Henry, were he here.
    Mar. Farewell, my lord. Good wishes, praise, and
    prayers   172
Shall Suffolk ever have of Margaret.   *She is going.*
    Suf. Farewell, sweet madam! but hark you, Mar-
    garet;
No princely commendations to my king?
    Mar. Such commendations as become a maid,
A virgin, and his servant, say to him.   177
    Suf. Words sweetly plac'd and modestly directed.
But madam, I must trouble you again,
No loving token to his majesty?   180
    Mar. Yes, my good lord; a pure unspotted heart,
Never yet taint with love, I send the king.
    Suf. And this withal.   *Kiss her.*
    Mar. That for thyself: I will not so presume,
To send such peevish tokens to a king.   185
        [*Exeunt Reignier and Margaret.*]
    Suf. O! wert thou for myself! But Suffolk, stay;
Thou mayst not wander in that labyrinth;
There Minotaurs and ugly treasons lurk.   188
Solicit Henry with her wondrous praise:
Bethink thee on her virtues that surmount

163 traffic: *business*   182 taint: *infected*   185 peevish: *silly*

And natural graces that extinguish art;
Repeat their semblance often on the seas,   192
That, when thou com'st to kneel at Henry's feet,
Thou mayst bereave him of his wits with wonder.

Exit.

Scene Four

[*Rouen*]

Enter York, Warwick, Shepherd, [with] Pucelle [guarded].

York. Bring forth that sorceress, condemn'd to burn.

Shep. Ah, Joan! this kills thy father's heart outright

Have I sought every country far and near,
And, now it is my chance to find thee out,   4
Must I behold thy timeless cruel death?
Ah, Joan! sweet daughter Joan, I'll die with thee.

Joan. Decrepit miser! base ignoble wretch!
I am descended of a gentler blood: 8
Thou art no father nor no friend of mine.

Shep. Out, out! My lords, an please you, 'tis not so;
I did beget her all the parish knows:
Her mother liveth yet, can testify   12
She was the first fruit of my bachelorship.

War. Graceless! wilt thou deny thy parentage?

York. This argues what her kind of life hath been:
Wicked and vile; and so her death concludes.   16

Shep. Fie, Joan, that thou wilt be so obstacle!

God knows, thou art a collop of my flesh;
And for thy sake have I shed many a tear:
Deny me not, I prithee, gentle Joan.   20
    Joan. Peasant, avaunt! You have suborn'd this
      man,
Of purpose to obscure my noble birth.
    Shep. 'Tis true, I gave a noble to the priest,
The morn that I was wedded to her mother.   24
Kneel down and take my blessing, good my girl.
Wilt thou not stoop? Now cursed be the time
Of thy nativity! I would the milk
Thy mother gave thee, when thou suck'dst her
    breast,   28
Had been a little ratsbane for thy sake!
Or else, when thou didst keep my lambs a-field,
I wish some ravenous wolf had eaten thee!
Dost thou deny thy father, cursed drab?   32
O! burn her, burn her! hanging is too good.   *Exit.*
    York. Take her away; for she hath liv'd too long,
To fill the world with vicious qualities.
    Joan. First, let me tell you whom you have con-
      demn'd: 36
Not me begotten of a shepherd swain,
But issu'd from the progeny of kings;
Virtuous and holy; chosen from above,
By inspiration of celestial grace,   40
To work exceeding miracles on earth.
I never had to do with wicked spirits:
But you,—that are polluted with your lusts,
Stain'd with the guiltless blood of innocents,   44
Corrupt and tainted with a thousand vices,—
Because you want the grace that others have,
You judge it straight a thing impossible

18 collop: *slice*   23 noble: *coin (worth 6 s. 8 d.)*

To compass wonders but by help of devils.　　48
No, misconceived! Joan of Arc hath been
A virgin from her tender infancy,
Chaste and immaculate in very thought;
Whose maiden blood, thus rigorously effus'd,　52
Will cry for vengeance at the gates of heaven
　　York. Ay, ay: away with her to execution!
　　War. And hark ye, sirs; because she is a maid,
Spare for no fagots, let there be enow:　　56
Place barrels of pitch upon the fatal stake,
That so her torture may be shortened.
　　Joan. Will nothing turn your unrelenting hearts?
Then, Joan, discover thine infirmity,　　60
That warranteth by law to be thy privilege.
I am with child, ye bloody homicides:
Murder not then the fruit within my womb,
Although ye hale me to a violent death.　　64
　　York. Now, heaven forfend! the holy maid with
　　　　child!
　　War. The greatest miracle that e'er ye wrought!
Is all your strict preciseness come to this?
　　York. She and the Dauphin have been jug-
　　　　gling:　　68
I did imagine what would be her refuge.
　　War. Well, go to; we will have no bastards live;
Especially since Charles must father it.
　　Joan. You are deceiv'd; my child is none of
　　　　his:　　72
It was Alençon that enjoy'd my love.
　　York. Alençon! that notorious Machiavel!
It dies an if it had a thousand lives.
　　Joan. O! give me leave, I have deluded you:　76

49 misconceived: *deluded ones*　　61 warranteth: *offers security*
74 that notorious Machiavel; *cf. n.*

'Twas neither Charles, nor yet the duke I nam'd,
But Reignier, King of Naples, that prevail'd.
   War. A married man: that's most intolerable.
   York. Why, here's a girl! I think she knows **not**
     well,   80
There were so many, whom she may accuse.
   War. It's sign she hath been liberal and free.
   York. And yet, forsooth, she is a virgin pure.
Strumpet, thy words condemn thy brat and thee: 84
Use no entreaty, for it is in vain.
   Joan. Then lead me hence; with whom I leave **my**
     curse:
May never glorious sun reflex his beams
Upon the country where you make abode;   88
But darkness and the gloomy shade of death
Environ you, till mischief and despair
Drive you to break your necks or hang yourselves!
                        Exit [*guarded*].
   York. Break thou in pieces and consume **to**
     ashes,   92
Thou foul accursed minister of hell!

               Enter Cardinal.

   Car. Lord regent, I do greet your excellence
With letters of commission from the king.
For know, my lords, the states of Christendom,   96
Mov'd with remorse of these outrageous broils,
Have earnestly implor'd a general peace
Betwixt our nation and the aspiring French;
And here at hand the Dauphin, and his train,   100
Approacheth to confer about some matter.
   York. Is all our travail turn'd to this effect?
After the slaughter of so many peers,

87 reflex: *cast*

So many captains, gentlemen, and soldiers,   104
That in this quarrel have been overthrown,
And sold their bodies for their country's benefit,
Shall we at last conclude effeminate peace?
Have we not lost most part of all the towns,   108
By treason, falsehood, and by treachery,
Our great progenitors had conquered?
O! Warwick, Warwick! I foresee with grief
The utter loss of all the realm of France.   112
    War. Be patient, York: if we conclude a peace,
It shall be with such strict and severe covenants
As little shall the Frenchmen gain thereby.

    Enter Charles, Alençon, Bastard, Reignier [and Others].

    Char. Since, lords of England, it is thus
      agreed,   116
That peaceful truce shall be proclaim'd in France,
We come to be informed by yourselves
What the conditions of that league must be.
    York. Speak, Winchester; for boiling choler
      chokes   120
The hollow passage of my poison'd voice,
By sight of these our baleful enemies.
    Car. Charles, and the rest, it is enacted thus:
That, in regard King Henry gives consent,   124
Of mere compassion and of lenity,
To ease your country of distressful war,
And suffer you to breathe in fruitful peace,
You shall become true liegemen to his crown: 128
And, Charles, upon condition thou wilt swear
To pay him tribute, and submit thyself,
Thou shalt be plac'd as viceroy under him,

121 poison'd; *cf. n.*

And still enjoy thy regal dignity.   132
    Alen. Must he be, then, as shadow of himself?
Adorn his temples with a coronet,
And yet, in substance and authority,
Retain but privilege of a private man?   136
This proffer is absurd and reasonless.
    Char. 'Tis known already that I am possess'd
With more than half the Gallian territories,
And therein reverenc'd for their lawful king: 140
Shall I, for lucre of the rest unvanquish'd,
Detract so much from that prerogative
As to be call'd but viceroy of the whole?
No, lord ambassador; I'll rather keep   144
That which I have than, coveting for more,
Be cast from possibility of all.
    York. Insulting Charles! hast thou by secret means
Us'd intercession to obtain a league,   148
And now the matter grows to compromise,
Stand'st thou aloof upon comparison?
Either accept the title thou usurp'st,
Of benefit proceeding from our king   152
And not of any challenge of desert,
Or we will plague thee with incessant wars.
    Reig. My lord, you do not well in obstinacy
To cavil in the course of this contract: 156
If once it be neglected, ten to one,
We shall not find like opportunity.
    Alen. [*Aside to Charles.*] To say the truth, it is
        your policy
To save your subjects from such massacre   160
And ruthless slaughters as are daily seen
By our proceeding in hostility;

141 lucre: *desire of gain*   149 grows to: *approaches*
150 comparison: *quibbling rhetoric*
152 Of benefit: *by way of bounty*

And therefore take this compact of a truce,
Although you break it when your pleasure serves.
  War. How sayst thou, Charles? shall our condition
    stand?   165
  Char. It shall;
Only reserv'd, you claim no interest
In any of our towns of garrison.
  York. Then swear allegiance to his majesty;   169
As thou art knight, never to disobey
Nor be rebellious to the crown of England,
Thou, nor thy nobles, to the crown of England.
          [*Charles, &c., give tokens of fealty.*]
So, now dismiss your army when ye please;   173
Hang up your ensigns, let your drums be still,
For here we entertain a solemn peace.   *Exeunt.*

Scene Five

[*London. A Room in the Palace*]

Enter Suffolk in conference with the King, Glouces-
ier, and Exeter.

  King. Your wondrous rare description, noble earl,
Of beauteous Margaret hath astonish'd me:
Her virtues, graced with external gifts
Do breed love's settled passions in my heart: 4
And like as rigour of tempestuous gusts
Provokes the mightiest hulk against the tide,
So am I driven by breath of her renown
Either to suffer shipwreck, or arrive   8
Where I may have fruition of her love.
  Suf. Tush! my good lord, this superficial tale
Is but a preface of her worthy praise:
The chief perfections of that lovely dame—   12

Had I sufficient skill to utter them—
Would make a volume of enticing lines,
Able to ravish any dull conceit:
And, which is more, she is not so divine,   16
So full replete with choice of all delights,
But with as humble lowliness of mind
She is content to be at your command:
Command, I mean, of virtuous chaste intents,   20
To love and honour Henry as her lord.
    King. And otherwise will Henry ne'er presume.
Therefore, my Lord Protector, give consent
That Margaret may be England's royal queen.   24
    Glo. So should I give consent to flatter sin.
You know, my lord, your highness is betroth'd
Unto another lady of esteem;
How shall we then dispense with that contract,   28
And not deface your honour with reproach?
    Suf. As doth a ruler with unlawful oaths;
Or one that, at a triumph having vow'd
To try his strength, forsaketh yet the lists   32
By reason of his adversary's odds.
A poor earl's daughter is unequal odds,
And therefore may be broke without offence.
    Glo. Why, what, I pray, is Margaret more than
      that?   36
Her father is no better than an earl.
Although in glorious titles he excel.
    Suf. Yes, my lord, her father is a king,
The King of Naples and Jerusalem;   40
And of such great authority in France
As his alliance will confirm our peace,
And keep the Frenchmen in allegiance.
    Glo. And so the Earl of Armagnac may do,   44

15 conceit: *imagination*   31. triumph: *tournament*

Because he is near kinsman unto Charles.
  Exe. Beside, his wealth doth warrant a liberal
    dower,
Where Reignier sooner will receive than give.
  Suf. A dower, my lords! disgrace not so your
    king,   48
That he should be so abject, base, and poor,
To choose for wealth and not for perfect love.
Henry is able to enrich his queen,
And not to seek a queen to make him rich: 52
So worthless peasants bargain for their wives,
As market-men for oxen, sheep, or horse.
Marriage is a matter of more worth
Than to be dealt in by attorneyship: 56
Not whom we will, but whom his Grace affects,
Must be companion of his nuptial bed;
And therefore, lords, since he affects her most
It most of all these reasons bindeth us,   60
In our opinions she should be preferr'd.
For what is wedlock forced, but a hell,
An age of discord and continual strife?
Whereas the contrary bringeth bliss,   64
And is a pattern of celestial peace.
Whom should we match with Henry, being a king,
But Margaret, that is daughter to a king?
Her peerless feature, joined with her birth,   68
Approves her fit for none but for a king:
Her valiant courage and undaunted spirit—
More than in women commonly is seen—
Will answer our hope in issue of a king;   72
For Henry, son unto a conqueror,
Is likely to beget more conquerors,

56 by attorneyship: *by the shrewd calculation of third parties*
68 feature: *form of body*

If with a lady of so high resolve
As is fair Margaret he be link'd in love.   76
Then yield, my lords; and here conclude with me
That Margaret shall be queen, and none but she.
   King. Whether it be through force of your report,
My noble lord of Suffolk, or for that   80
My tender youth was never yet attaint
With any passion of inflaming love,
I cannot tell; but this I am assur'd,
I feel such sharp dissension in my breast,   84
Such fierce alarums both of hope and fear,
As I am sick with working of my thoughts.
Take, therefore, shipping; post, my lord, to France;
Agree to any covenants, and procure   88
That Lady Margaret do vouchsafe to come
To cross the seas to England and be crown'd
King Henry's faithful and anointed queen:
For your expenses and sufficient charge,   92
Among the people gather up a tenth.
Be gone, I say; for till you do return
I rest perplexed with a thousand cares.
And you, good uncle, banish all offence: 96
If you do censure me by what you were,
Not what you are, I know it will excuse
This sudden execution of my will.
And so, conduct me, where from company   100
I may revolve and ruminate my grief.   *Exit.*
   Glo. Ay, grief, I fear me, both at first and last.
            Exit Gloucester [with Exeter].
   Suf. Thus Suffolk hath prevail'd; and thus he goes,
As did the youthful Paris once to Greece;   104
With hope to find the like event in love,

---

92 charge: *money to spend*   93 gather up a tenth; *cf. n.*
100 from company: *unaccompanied*   105 event: *outcome*

But prosper better than the Trojan did.
Margaret shall now be queen, and rule the king;
But I will rule both her, the king, and realm.　　108

Exit.

FINIS.

NOTES

The First Part of Henry the Sixth. The numeral is invariably spelled 'Sixt' in the old editions, the new form of the word being very rare in Shakespeare's time. So 'fift' for 'fifth,' as for instance in the opening stage direction and in line 6 below.

I. i. 1. *Hung be the heavens with black.* This meteorological reference receives added point from the Elizabethan practice of draping the stage in black when a tragedy was to be acted. Cf., for example, lines 74, 75 of the Induction to *A Warning for Fair Women* (perhaps by Thomas Heywood), printed in 1599:

> 'The stage is hung with black, and I perceive
> The auditors prepar'd for Tragedy.'

The play cited was acted by Shakespeare's company.

I. i. 50. *marish.* Pope's emendation for the *Nourish* (i.e., nurse ?) of the Folios, which many modern editors retain.

I. i. 60, 61. These lines illustrate the freedom with which the play everywhere alters historic fact. Two of the places named, Orleans and Poitiers, were not in English possession. The others were not lost till periods varying from seven to nearly thirty years after the date represented in the scene. Possibly we should understand that the first Messenger is reporting exaggerated rumors. His statement in regard to Orleans is contradicted by what the third Messenger says in line 157 (cf. also line 111).

I. i. 92. Another anachronism. The crowning of Charles VII at Rheims, the culmination of Joan of Arc's triumphs, actually occurred seven years later (July 12, 1429). Charles had, however, been

crowned at Poitiers in 1422. The Bastard of
Orleans, mentioned in the next line, was Jean, Count
Dunois (1402-1468), illegitimate son of the Duke of
Orleans and first cousin of Charles VII. He was one
of the finest soldiers of his age, and is introduced in
a conspicuous rôle in Schiller's play, *Die Jungfrau
von Orleans,* as well as in Voltaire's earlier mock-
heroic, *La Pucelle d'Orléans.*

I. i. 110, 111. *The tenth of August last . . . the
siege of Orleans.* These lines and those which follow
describe the Battle of Patay (June 18, 1429), of
which another account is introduced in IV. i. 19-26.
The general issue of the battle is correctly given and
it is rightly said to have followed the British retire-
ment from the siege of Orleans (May 8, 1429); but
the allusion to Patay in the present lines is out of
place, since the raising of the siege of Orleans is
portrayed in a later part of the play (I. v and vi).

I. i. 116. *wanted pikes to set before his archers.*
The military tactics of the day directed that the
archers, often stationed on the flanks of the army,
should be protected from charges of cavalry by rows
of pikes fixed in the ground, points outward. Holinshed's statement is that the English set their pikes
(stakes) before the archers in the usual way, but had
no time afterwards to arrange their line of battle.

I. i. 124. *flew.* The Folios have the easy mis-
print 'slew' (with long s) which a very few editors
are quixotic enough to champion.

I. i. 131. *Sir John Fastolfe.* This episode of
Fastolfe's cowardice is four times employed in the
play. Cf. I. iv. 35-37; III. ii. 104-109; IV. i. 9-47.
Modern historians represent Fastolfe as a general of
distinction and of unblemished valor but the chroniclers of Shakespeare's day accepted the libel incor-
porated in the play. The chief interest of the figure
here is his connection with the great Falstaff of the
Henry IV plays. It is to be noted that the early

editions of the present play invariably call Fastolfe
Sir John Falstaffe, a fact which suggests that, in the
minds of the editors of the First Folio, at least, the
two were identified. J. B. Henneman (*Publ. Mod.
Lang. Assoc.*, xv, 1900) gives a number of reasons
for assuming that when Shakespeare chose the name
Falstaff for the fat knight of *Henry IV* and *The
Merry Wives of Windsor* (originally called Sir John
Oldcastle), he was actuated by reminiscence of
Fastolfe in the present play. L. W. V. Harcourt
identifies Falstaff with another Sir John Fastolf. See
the articles on Fastolf mentioned in Appendix E.

I. i. 132. *in the vaward,—plac'd behind.* Almost
a contradiction in terms, which editors have sought to
harmonize by emendation ('rearward' for *vaward*)
or by casuistry. The most reasonable interpretation
is perhaps that of H. C. Hart: 'Fastolfe was in support (placed behind) of the vanguard, which was
probably led by Talbot himself.'

I. i. 148. *His ransom there is none but I shall pay.*
An ambiguous line which may be paraphrased in two
ways: (1) 'I will pay any ransom that may be
named'; (2) 'I alone will pay his ransom,' i.e., leave
it to me.

I. i. 154. *Saint George's feast.* Properly, April
23 (the day of Shakespeare's death and traditionally
his birthday). Bonfires in honor of St. George, however, would be appropriate on any day of English
victory.

I. i. 162. *your oaths to Henry sworn.* Holinshed
relates how Henry V on his deathbed admonished the
Dukes of Bedford and Gloucester and the Earls of
Salisbury and Warwick never to make a treaty with
the Dauphin by which any part of France might be
relinquished, and how he commanded Bedford as
Regent of France 'with fire and sword to persecute
the Dolphin, till he had either brought him to reason
and obeisance, or else to driue and expell him out of

the realme of France.' He adds: 'The noble men present promised to obscrue his precepts, and to performe his desires.'

I. i. 170. *Eltham.* A village nine miles southeast of London, on the road to Dartford and Canterbury. The Palace, of which picturesque remains still exist, was a favorite residence of the English sovereigns from the thirteenth to the middle of the sixteenth century. In line 176, *steal* is a modern emendation (by Mason) for 'send' of the Folios. Though not inevitable, the change is supported by the rime, frequent at the close of scenes, and it has been adopted in most recent texts. On the other hand, support for the Folio reading may perhaps be found in the words of Holinshed, who refers to Winchester's alleged purpose 'to set hand on the kings person, and to haue remooued him from Eltham, the place that he was in, to Windsor.'

I. ii. 1. *Mars his true moving.* The planet Mars has a very eccentric orbit, and his apparently irregular course puzzled astronomers till explained by Kepler in 1609. Editors have noted a strikingly similar allusion in Thomas Nashe's preface to *Have with you to Saffron Walden* (1596): 'you are as ignorant . . . as the Astronomers are in the true mouings of *Mars,* which to this day they could neuer attaine too.' (McKerrow's Nashe, iii. 20.)

I. ii. 56. *the nine sibyls of old Rome.* The Cumæan Sibyl offered King Tarquin nine books. The poet has transferred the number to the sibyls themselves, of whom various numbers (but not nine) are reckoned.

I. ii. 105. *the sword of Deborah.* Cf. Judges, chapters 4 and 5.

I. ii. 110. *Excellent Pucelle, if thy name be so.* Holinshed's Chronicle introduces Joan of Arc as 'Ione Are' or more fully, 'Ione de Are, Pusell de dieu.' The Folio text of the play usually refers to

her simply as *Pucelle* (spelled 'Puzel' or 'Pucell').
The stage direction after line 63 of this scene calls
her 'Ioane Puzel,' that after line 103 'Ioane de
Puzel' (so also in I. vi. 3 and V. iii. S. d.). In II. i
and V. iv she appears as 'Ioane,' but is only twice
called Joan of Arc ('Acre' or 'Aire' in the Folio; cf.
II. ii. 20 and V. iv. 49). Mr. Fleay attempted to
find in these differences of name a clue to the play's
authorship.

I. ii. 131. *Saint Martin's summer.* Summer in
the midst of autumn. The reference is to the unsea-
sonably warm weather often occurring about St.
Martin's Day (November 11).

I. ii. 138, 139. The allusion is to a common but
probably unhistoric story recorded in Plutarch's Life
of Cæsar. During the war with Pompey, when the
latter's navy commanded the sea, Cæsar embarked
on a small pinnace incognito 'as if he had bene some
poore man of meane condition,' with the idea of
crossing to his army at Brundisium. A storm arose
and the commander of the vessel ordered his men to
put back. 'Cæsar, hearing that, straight discouered
himselfe vnto the Maister of the pynnase, who at the
first was amazed when he saw him: but Cæsar then
taking him by the hand sayd vnto him, Good fellow,
be of good cheare, and forwards hardily, feare not,
for thou hast Cæsar & his fortune with thee.' (North's
translation, 1579.) Peele mentions the episode in a
similar manner in his *Farewell* to Norris and Drake
(1589):

> 'and let me say
> To you, my mates, as Cæsar said to his,
> Striving with Neptune's hills; you bear, quoth he,
> Cæsar, and Cæsar's fortune in your ships.'

I. ii. 140. *Was Mahomet inspired with a dove?*
This alludes to a trick ascribed to Mahomet by several
Elizabethan writers. Thomas Nashe has two refer-
ences to it, and Nashe's most recent editor quotes the

following from an earlier work, *Strange Things out of
Seb. Munster* (1574): 'For he [Mahomet] accustomed
and taught a Doue to be fedde and fetch meate [i.e.,
food] at his eares, the which Doue his moste subtile
and craftye maister called the holy Ghoste. He
preached openly, and made his bragges like a most
lying villen that this Doue did shew vnto him the
most secrete counsel of God, as often as the simple
fowle did flye vnto his eares for nourishment.' (Mc-
Kerrow's Nashe, iv. 200.)

I. ii. 142. *Helen, the mother of great Constantine.*
The reputed discoverer of the True Cross. Two
frescoes representing this legend adorned the Guild
Chapel at Stratford in Shakespeare's time. See
reproductions in Ward, *Shakespeare's Town and
Times,* p. 33.

I. ii. 143. *Saint Philip's daughters.* Referred to
in Acts 21. 9 as 'virgins, which did prophesy.'

I. iii. 19. *The Cardinal of Winchester.* Editors
have pointed out that the mention of Winchester's
cardinalate in this scene is inconsistent with the fact
that he is represented as only just made cardinal in
V. i. 28 ff. and is called bishop in III. i. 53 and IV. i.
1. Winchester became cardinal in 1427, but the
chroniclers report that there had been much previous
talk of his probable elevation.

I. iii. 22. *Woodvile.* Holinshed records that when
Gloucester wished to enter the Tower, 'Richard
Wooduile esquier (hauing at that time the charge of
the keeping of the Tower) refused his desire; and
kept the same Tower against him vndulie and against
reason, by the commandement of my said lord of
Winchester.' Woodvile became a person of great
consequence upon the marriage, nearly forty years
later, of his daughter to Edward IV, and in 1466 was
created Earl Rivers.

I. iii. 34. *Thou that contriv'dst to murder our
dead lord.* The fourth of five charges brought

against Winchester by Gloucester (in 1426) relates
to the former's alleged complicity in an attempt to
murder the Prince of Wales, later Henry V.   The
same scandal has been more obscurely insinuated by
Gloucester in I. i. 33, 34.

I. iii. 35.   The disorderly houses on the Southwark bank of the Thames were under the control of
the Bishop of Winchester and paid him a revenue.
The proximity of these houses to the Rose Theatre,
where this play appears to have been first acted (and
to the later Globe), doubtless gave point to the
allusion.

I. iii. 39.   *This be Damascus, be thou cursed Cain.*
Several popular mediæval works (Mandeville's
Travels, Higden's *Polychronicon*) gave currency to
the belief that Abel was slain on the site of Damascus.

I. iv. 23-56.   This passage involves several an-
achronisms.   Salisbury's mortal wound was received
at Orleans in October, 1428.   Talbot was captured at
Patay in June, 1429, and was not released by ex-
change with Santrailles till 1433.

I. iv. 95.   *Plantagenet.*   Montacute, not Plantagenet, was Salisbury's name.   Furthermore, the appella-
tion Plantagenet was not adopted by the English
royal family till after Salisbury's death.   It first
appears in public records in 1460, being revived by
one of the characters in this play, Richard Duke of
York, as a means of expressing superiority of descent
over the Lancastrian line (cf. D. N. B. s. v. Plantagenet).

like thee.   The reading of the First Folio, meaning
'I will be as unconcernedly remorseless as you have
been.'   The next line carries with it a subordinate
reminiscence of the well-known story of Nero, which
led the later Folios to alter *like thee* to 'Nero-like
will.'   Malone then blended the two readings into the
vapid 'like thee, Nero,' a perversion which nearly all
modern editors have unfortunately accepted.

I. iv. 107. *dolphin or dogfish.* Dogfish, a small shark, was commonly used as an opprobrious epithet. Dolphin is the invariable form of the French title Dauphin in the early editions of the play. Modern editors substitute the present spelling in all cases except this, where the pun requires retention of the older form. It should be remarked that the Dauphin of the play was from the legitimist French point of view King of France (Charles VII) through the entire course of the action, since the death of his father, Charles VI, occurred only two months after that of Henry V. The English, however, ignored Charles VII's pretensions to the throne and continued to employ his old title.

I. v. 6. *Blood will I draw on thee, thou art a witch.* Johnson asserted the existence of a superstition that 'he that could draw the witch's blood was free from her power'; but no confirmation of this has apparently been found in Elizabethan literature.

I. v. 14 S. d. Joan here goes from the lower to the upper stage of the Elizabethan theatre, lines 15-18 being spoken from the upper or balcony stage.

I. v. 21. *like Hannibal.* The allusion is perhaps to the stratagem recorded by Livy (bk. xxii. c. 16, 17); Hannibal extricated his forces from an unfavorable position by driving against Fabius's army during the night two thousand oxen with blazing fagots tied to their horns.

I. v. 28. *tear the lions out of England's coat.* The armorial dress of the kings of England was embroidered with three lions (or leopards).

I. vi. 4. *Astræa's daughter.* That is, daughter of Justice, in allusion to the myth that Astræa forsook the world when it became corrupt, and carried her divine scales to the constellation of Libra. Spenser develops the legend elaborately at the opening of the fifth book of the *Fairy Queen;* and Peele's *Descensus Astrææ* turns it into a pageant in honor of the installation of a new lord mayor of London in 1591.

I. vi. 6. *Adonis' gardens*. What these were in classic literature has been acrimoniously disputed, but a beautiful and extended description, which perhaps inspired the present line, is given by Spenser, *Fairy Queen*, bk. iii. canto vi.

I. vi. 22. *Rhodope's of Memphis*. One of the most beautiful pyramids was said to have been built by Rhodope, a Greek courtesan who married the king of Memphis. The reading in the text is a conjecture of Capell for 'Rhodophes or Memphis' of the Folios.

I. vi. 25. *the rich-jewell'd coffer of Darius*. Alexander the Great is said to have kept Homer's poems under his pillow at night and during the day to have carried them 'in the rich iewel cofer of Darius, lately before vanquished by him in battaile.' (Puttenham, *Art of English Poesie*, 1589.)

II. i. 7 S. d. *dead march*. The dead march is in honor of Salisbury, whose body is carried with the army. Cf. line 4 of the next scene. (Hart.)

II. i. 8. *redoubted Burgundy*. Philip the Good, Duke of Burgundy, had been alienated from the Dauphin by the treacherous murder of his father in 1419. He was the ally of the English from the time of the treaty of Troyes (1420) till 1435. He was the second cousin of Charles VII and father of the famous Charles the Bold.

II. i. 38 S. d. *The French leap o'er the walls in their shirts*. This entire episode, which the dramatist has transferred to Orleans, is based upon an incident that really occurred in May, 1428 (a year before the relief of Orleans), at Le Mans in the adjacent province of Maine. Holinshed, following earlier chroniclers, records that the Frenchmen, surprised by an early morning counter-attack, 'got vp in their shirts, and lept ouer the walles.'

II. iii. 6. *As Scythian Tomyris by Cyrus' death.*
The story of Herodotus is that Tomyris, Queen of
the Massagetæ, led her troops to battle after her
husband's death, slew Cyrus the Great (B. C. 529),
and in scorn of his bloodthirstiness dropped his
severed head into a wine skin filled with blood. Compare the countess's address to Talbot in line 34.

II. iii. 22. *this is a child, a silly dwarf.* The
countess exaggerates greatly. Talbot was eighty
years of age when he fell in battle, and the exami-
nation of his bones, when they were exhumed in 1874,
showed that he could not have been undersized. 'The
bones generally were remarkably well developed, and
had evidently belonged to a muscular man.'

II. iv. 6. *Or else was wrangling Somerset in th'
error?* Capell changed *error* to 'right' and Rolfe,
retaining the old text, wished to interpret *else* as 'in
other words.' Neither, probably, is justified. Richard's apparent alternatives amount to the same thing.
From craft or from impetuosity he leaves the hearers
to whom he appeals but one answer. It is 'heads, I
win; tails, Somerset loses.'

II. iv. 7. *Faith, I have been a truant in the law.*
Shakespeare brilliantly imagines the quarrel of the
roses to have started among a group of young aristo-
crats, studying law in the Temple.

II. iv. 81. *the yeoman.* Somerset's slur is explained in his next speech. The execution of Plantagenet's father for treason (as recorded in the play
of *Henry V*) deprived his heir of all titles of
nobility. Lionel of Clarence, third son of Edward
III, was not the grandfather, as Warwick states in
line 83, but the great-great-grandfather of Plantagenet. See the genealogical table on next page.

II. iv. 96. *attached, not attainted.* Literally,
arrested, but not formally condemned, as by bill of
attainder, to the legal consequences of treason. It
is evident that the speaker is splitting hairs, but it

The following table illustrates the relationships of the various members of the English royal family.

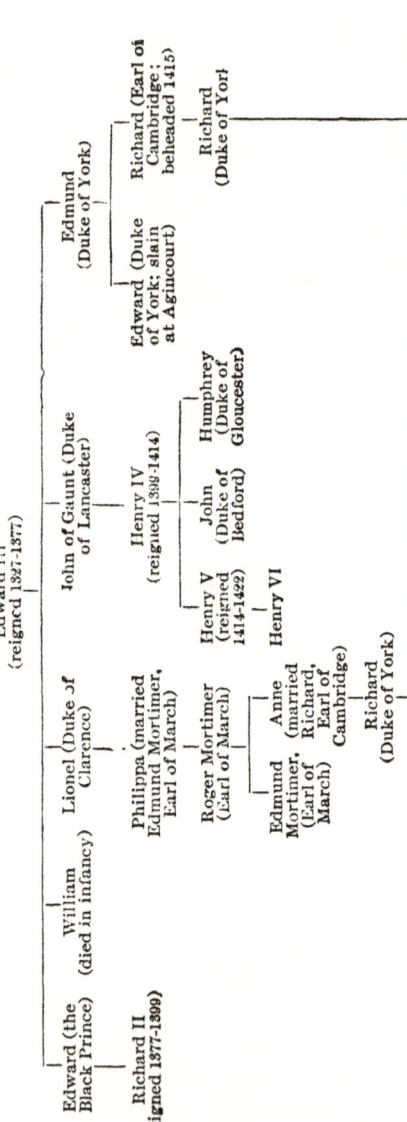

Somerset (John, 1st Duke of Somerset, 1403–1444) was the grandson of John of Gaunt, his father and the Bishop of Winchester (cf. III. i. 42) being both illegitimate sons of that prince.

does appear that Richard was permitted to succeed
to his inheritances without the formal restoration to
his blood which the play represents (III. i. 148 ff.).
See D. N. B.

II. v. 6. *Nestor-like aged, in an age of care.* That
is, trebly aged by care. 'The care that has afflicted
my life has made me as old as Nestor' (who lived
through three mortal lifetimes).

II. v. 7. *Edmund Mortimer.* The poet adopts
without essential alteration the statement of the
chroniclers. Holinshed says: 'Edmund Mortimer, the
last earle of March of that name (which long time
had beene restreined from his libertie . . .) deceassed
without issue; whose inheritance descended to the
lord Richard Plantagenet.' Modern commentators
point out that the chronicles, and with them Shakespeare, are wrong, since this Mortimer died in freedom in 1424. Apparently, they confused Edmund
Mortimer, Earl of March, with his cousin, Sir John
Mortimer, who after long captivity was executed in
the same year (1424). It is evident, moreover, from
the use of the word 'mother' rather than 'grandmother' in line 74, that Shakespeare further confuses
Edmund Mortimer, Earl of March, with an older
Edmund Mortimer, his uncle, just as he does in the
first part of *Henry IV.* (See note on I. iii. 145, 146
of that play in the present edition.)

II. v. 96. *the rest I wish thee gather.* Probably
gather is used in the well-authenticated Shakespearean sense of 'infer,' and Mortimer desires cautiously
to remind his nephew of the full significance of his
heirship; namely, the claim to the crown that it
carries with it.

II. v. 129. 'Or make my injuries an instrument for
attaining my ambition.' The Folios read 'will' instead
of *ill*, the latter being one of Theobald's convincing
emendations.

III. i. The historical place of this scene was Leicester, where Parliament met in 1426 (three years before the relief of Orleans depicted in Act I). Line 77 shows, however, that the dramatist thought of the events as occurring in London. King Henry, who plays a precocious part in the scene, was actually in his fifth year.

III. i. 22, 23. Gloucester's third charge against Winchester, as reported by the chroniclers, was that he had put men at arms and archers in ambush at the Southwark end of London Bridge, with intent to slay the Protector if he attempted to pass that way to the young king at Eltham. The reference to the trap laid at the Tower alludes of course to the incident dramatized in I. iii.

III. i. 51. *Rome . . . Roam.* The words were not identical in sound. Elsewhere in Shakespeare *Rome* rimes with 'doom,' 'groom,' 'room,'—words which have not essentially changed their pronunciation, while *roam* has presumably the vowel sound in modern 'broad.' Probably the pun in the present line was consciously inexact. Otherwise one might argue that Shakespeare was not its author.

III. i. 63. *enter talk.* On the precedent of the participle *entertalking* in Golding's translation of Ovid (1565-67), Hart changed this phrase to a single word: *entertalk.* The New English Dictionary does not recognize the word.

III. i. 78-85. This reference to the use of pebble stones, when weapons were forbidden the adherents of the contending noblemen, appears to show that the author of the scene had recourse to the ancient chronicler Fabyan. The episode is not mentioned by Holinshed.

III. i. 163-165. Richard Plantagenet inherited the earldom of Cambridge from his father and the dukedom of York from his father's elder brother, who had died (at Agincourt; cf. *Henry V,* IV. vi.) without

.ssue. To these great estates were added by inheritance from his mother's side the titles of the Morti-
ners, Earls of March.

III. i. 178, 179. King Henry's voyage to France
occurred at the close of 1431, five years after the
Parliament of Leicester which furnished the material
for the opening portion of this scene.

III. i. 185 S. d. *Sennet.* A sennet was a trumpet
signal to mark the approach or departure of a procession.

III. i. 194. *that fatal prophecy.* The prophecy
was very well known in Shakespeare's time—more so,
doubtless, than in Henry V's. Holinshed thus reports it: 'The king, being certified [of the birth of
his son at Windsor] gaue God thanks . . . But,
when he heard reported the place of his natiuitie,
were it that he [had been] warned by some prophesie,
or had some foreknowledge, or else iudged himselfe
of his sonnes fortune, he said vnto the lord Fitz
Hugh, his trustie chamberleine, these words: "My
lord, I Henrie, borne at Monmouth, shall small time
reigne, & much get; and Henrie, borne at Windsore,
shall long reigne, and all loose: but as God will, so
be it."'

III. ii. S. d. The story of the capture of Rouen
is apocryphal. This city remained in the hands of
the English till 1449, eighteen years after Joan of
Arc had been burned there. The particular stratagem
here related may have been suggested by two different anecdotes found in the chroniclers, one referring
to the capture of the castle of Cornill (Corville ?) by
the English, the other to the capture of Le Mans by
the French.

III. ii. 22. *Where.* This is Rowe's emendation,
adopted regularly by subsequent editors. The Folios
read *Here,* which may well be defended: Joan's signal
is not to distinguish the safest passageway, but to

indicate the practicability of that by which she entered.

III. ii. 28. *Talbonites.* A derivative formed from a Latinized version of Talbot's name: Talbo, Talbonis (though Talbottus is the form used by Camden). Modern editors seem all to accept Theobald's cacophonous emendation, 'Talbotites.' N. E. D. recognizes neither word.

III. ii. 40. *the pride of France.* Compare *the pride of Gallia* (IV. vi. 15). These sonorous phrases mean hardly more than 'the French.' They are echoes of Marlowe, who had rung the changes upon 'the pride of Asia,' 'the pride of Græcia.'

III. ii. 40 S. d. *Alençon.* The Folios make Reignier enter here, not Alençon, and for the speaker's name in lines 23 and 33 above they have '*Reig.,*' not '*Alen.*' This, probably, is only a careless slip. It is not at all likely that Alençon and Reignier were both on the walls (upper stage) in addition to Charles, Joan, and the Bastard; and the three cases just noted are the only mentions of Reignier in this scene or the next.

III. ii. 50. *good grey-beard.* John, Duke of Bedford, third son of Henry IV, was only about forty-five years of age when he died in 1435. Here his death is antedated, being thrown back into the lifetime of Joan, whom he actually survived by four years, and his age is greatly exaggerated. Bedford is called by Hume 'the most accomplished prince of his age, a skilful politician, as well as a good general.' Shakespeare, in the second part of *Henry IV*, paints an unfavorable portrait of him in his youth, as Prince John of Lancaster.

III. ii. 81. *And as his father here was conqueror.* Henry V captured Rouen in 1518, after a long siege. Shakespeare's play of *Henry V* does not allude to this conquest.

III. ii. 82, 83. Holinshed tells how Richard I

'willed his heart to be conueied vnto Rouen, and there buried; in testimonie of the loue which he had euer borne vnto that citie for the stedfast faith and tried loialtie at all times found in the citizens there.'

III. ii. 95, 96. This story is told of Uther Pendragon (King Arthur's father) by Geoffrey of Monmouth, followed by Malory (I. iv) and by Harding. Holinshed's later compilation refers the exploit to Pendragon's brother. Marlowe's Tamburlaine similarly puts his foes to flight when afflicted with mortal sickness.

III. iii. 19, 20. Burgundy's actual abandonment of the English for the French occurred several years after Joan's death. Knight, however, called attention to a letter (which the authors of the play can hardly have known), written by Joan to Burgundy on the very day of Charles VII's coronation at Rheims (July 17, 1429). In this she makes use of much the same arguments as in the scene before us.

III. iii. 69-73. The facts, as accurately stated by the chroniclers, are here greatly distorted. The Duke of Orleans, captured at Agincourt in 1415, was kept prisoner in England till 1440. His release thus took place five years after Burgundy's defection, and is stated to have been largely by reason of Burgundy's efforts.

III. iii. 85. *Done like a Frenchman,* etc. The apparent inconsistency of this line in Joan's mouth has been much discussed. It is not in character, but is a clear appeal from the original author of the play to the prejudice of his audience. Hart thinks that Joan, as an inhabitant of Lorraine, 'would not hesitate to speak thus of the French people.' But if Lorraine was not strictly French, neither was Burgundy. Warburton suggested that the line was 'an offering of the poet to his royal mistress's resentment for Henry the Fourth's last great turn in religion. in the year 1598,' i.e., his renunciation of Protestantism.

III. iv. 18. *I do remember how my father said.*
Malone acutely cited this line in defence of his
contention that this play is not by Shakespeare or
by the author of the early versions of *2* and *3 Henry
VI*. The author of the present play, he argued, did
not know that Henry VI was a nine-months' infant
when his father died. Shakespeare did know this (cf.
Epilogue to *Henry V*), and so did the author of the
True Tragedy (*3 Henry VI*), neither of whom could
therefore have written Part I. On the other hand,
it might be explained that we have here one of
Shakespeare's purposeful tamperings with dramatic
time. There is an advantage in making the King
appear older than he really was without reminding
the reader that the whole long time from infancy to
maturity has elapsed since the play began (with the
funeral of Henry V).

III. iv. 26. *We here create you Earl of Shrewsbury.* Talbot was thus ennobled in 1442, eleven years
after the coronation of Henry, to which the king in-
vites him in the next line.

III. iv. 38, 39. 'By the ancient common law . . .
striking in the king's court of justice, or drawing a
sword therein, was a capital felony.' (Blackstone.)

IV. i. Henneman notes the 'curious relation' which
this scene bears to the previous one (III. iv). 'Both
have the King in Paris; both have identically the
same actors; both have the same two situations, viz.,
Talbot's interview with the King, and the quarrel of
Vernon and Basset, the followers respectively of York
and Somerset. But the second scene is developed
far beyond the former, and the spirit of the two is
equally different. One is condensed and compressed;
the other elaborated and heightened by fresh details.'
Annotators have observed that when Henry VI was

crowned at Paris (1431), Talbot was still a prisoner
to the French, Exeter was dead, and Gloucester in
England serving as the King's lieutenant.

IV. i. 19. *Patay.* The Folios erroneously print
'Poictiers,' doubtless from confusion in the composi-
tor's mind with the Black Prince's great victory at
Poitiers seventy-three years before (1356). For the
battle of Patay, cf. note on I. i. 110, 111.

IV. i. 181 S. d. *Flourish.* Modern editors place
this 'Flourish' in the stage direction following line
173, after the exit of the king. It probably belongs
there.

IV. ii. A lapse of twenty-two years, from Henry's
coronation (1431) to Talbot's last campaign (1453),
is covered rather skilfully by the concluding portion
of the previous scene.

IV. ii. 10, 11. *my three attendants, Lean famine,
quartering steel, and climbing fire.* These words furnish a significant parallel to those in the Prologue
preceding Act I of *Henry V*, lines 6-8:

'and at his heels,
Leash'd in like hounds, should famine, sword, and fire
Crouch for employment.'

The figures are not identical, but each bears the
Shakespearean stamp, and both (more particularly
that in the present play) are reminiscent of a speech
which the chroniclers report Henry V to have made
to the besieged citizens of Rouen.

IV. iii. 47. *vulture of sedition.* A figurative allusion to the vulture which fed in the bosom of the
bound Prometheus.

IV. iii. 50. *scarce cold conqueror.* Henry V had
been dead thirty-one years when Talbot fell, but the
hyperbole is dramatically effective and tends in a very
Shakespearean way to give cohesion and the sense
of rapid movement.

IV. iv.   Modern editors designate this scene as
occurring on 'Other Plains in Gascony,' but it is evident that there is no change of place, since Lucy
continues upon the stage.   (The later Folios inserted
an 'Exit' after the last line of scene iii, but there is
none in the original text.)

IV. iv. 13. *Whither, my lord?* Lucy impatiently
echoes the question, which he scorns to answer. His
concern is with the person from whom, not the one
to whom, he is sent.

IV. vi. 44. *On that advantage.* Perhaps this can
be construed in the sense of 'for the sake of that advantage,' i.e., personal safety. In that case the
phrase must be understood as modifying *fly* in line 46.
This, however, is strained, and it may be better to
interpret 'Fie on that advantage' and supply an excla-
mation point for the comma at the end of line 45.

IV. vii. 63-71. *Great Earl of Washford,* etc.
Great interest attaches to this list of Talbot's titles.
No source for it has been discovered earlier than an
epitaph of Talbot printed in 1599 (in Richard
Crompton's *Mansion of Magnanimitie*), which runs
thus: 'here lieth the right noble knight, Iohn Talbott,
Earle of Shrewsbury, Washford, Waterford, and
Valence, Lord Talbot of Goodrige, and Vrchengfield,
Lord Strange of the blacke Meere, Lord Verdon of
Alton, Lord Crumwell of Wingfield, Lord Louetoft
of Worsop, Lord Furniuall of Sheffield, Lord Faulcon-
brige, knight of the most noble order of S. George,
S. Michaell, and the Golden fleece, Great Marshall
to king Henry the sixt of his realme of France . . .'
It will be seen that this agrees almost verbatim with
the text of the play, the only alterations in the latter
being the omission of one title and the addition of
a few words for metrical purposes. The prose of
the epitaph is therefore treated in the very manner
in which in the Roman plays Shakespeare treated
much of the prose of North's Plutarch, and the whole

passage has a strong Shakespearean flavor. Are we, then, to infer that Shakespeare made his alteration of the play not earlier than 1599, at about the time when he was writing *Henry V?* See Appendix on The History of the Play.

IV. vii. 89, 94. *'em.* The First Folio has 'him' in both cases, owing probably to misreading of 'hem' (i.e., *'em*) in the manuscript.

V. i. 1, 2. Two events, separated by a considerable time, are here combined: the intervention of the Emperor Sigismund and the Pope in 1435 to secure peace in France, and the proposal to marry Henry to the daughter of the Count of Armagnac in 1442. Both these incidents long antedated Talbot's death.

V. iii. 1. *The regent conquers.* Historically, Bedford was regent of France when Joan was captured in 1430, but York is of course intended both here and in IV. vi. 2 (cf. IV. i. 162, 163).

V. iii. 6. *monarch of the north.* Evil spirits were identified with various quarters of the compass, particularly the east and the north.

V. iii. 29 S. d. *Burgundy and York fight.* So the Folio editions. Modern editors make the fight take place between Joan and York, but without justification. Joan's power has now disappeared and her part is passive. Probably the *Exit* after line 29, though in the old texts, should be omitted, leaving Joan a spectator of the fight which follows.

V. iii. 63. *Twinkling another counterfeited beam.* That is, each twinkling beam, reflected by the water, seems doubled.

V. iii. 68. *is she not here?* This is the reading of the First Folio. The second, third, and fourth, apparently troubled by the fact that the line has but four feet, added 'thy prisoner' after *here,* and they have been followed by most modern editors, though the words supplied are quite otiose.

V. iii. 75. [*Aside*]. This stage direction, here
and in the following lines, is added by modern editors.
It will be observed that the speeches so marked are
only partially inaudible.

V. iii. 78, 79. A quasi-proverbial saying, found
in *Titus Andronicus* (II. i. 82, 83) and elsewhere.

V. iv. S. d. *Rouen.* Modern editors place this
scene at the 'Camp of the Duke of York, in Anjou,'
to connect it with the previous scene which they put
'Before Angiers.' Really there are here two scenes,
which, save for the authority of convention, ought
to be separated. The first, dealing with the death of
Joan in 1431, must be localized at Rouen. The second,
beginning at line 94, dramatizes the peace negotia-
tions which took place at Arras in 1435. With the
meeting between Joan and her father should be con-
trasted the different treatment of the same theme in
Act IV, scene xi, of Schiller's play. (Schiller, for
dramatic effect, places the father's denunciation at
Rheims immediately after the coronation of Charles
VII.)

V. iv. 74. *Alençon! that notorious Machiavel.* The
reference to Machiavelli (1469-1527) is an anachronism in York's mouth, but no modern figure was more
familiarly talked of by the Elizabethans. By them
he was regarded as the symbol of heartless ambition.
It is very likely that in coupling Alençon with
Machiavel the author intended a by-reference to the
notorious Duke of Alençon who came a wooing to
Queen Elizabeth in 1579 and aroused the violent
antipathy of her subjects.

V. iv. 121. *poison'd.* This can perhaps be in-
terpreted to mean that the throat poisoned by choler
chokes the voice. Many editors, however, and
with good reason, accept Theobald's emendation,
'prison'd.'

V. v. 93. *Among the people gather up a tenth.*
Levy a special tax of ten per cent on incomes. Suf-

folk's levy, however, is stated to have been a fifteenth, not a tenth, and in the first scene of the second part of the play we have the correct figure:

> 'That Suffolk should demand a whole fifteenth
> For costs and charges in transporting her!'
> *(2 Henry VI,* I. i. 134, 135.)

APPENDIX A

The historical material in *1 Henry VI* is arranged with a total disregard to chronology, as the notes on various passages indicate. The earliest event portrayed is the funeral of Henry V on November 7, 1422; the latest the recovery of Talbot's body after his death on July 17, 1453. In some parts, the play is certainly based upon Shakespeare's favorite authority, the second edition of Raphael Holinshed's Chronicle of England (1587). Close following of this book is evident when the introduction of Joan of Arc (I. ii. 46-150) is compared with Holinshed's words: 'In time of this siege at Orleance . . . vnto Charles the Dolphin, at Chinon, as he was in verie great care and studie how to wrestle against the English nation . . . was caried a yoong wench of an eighteene yeeres old, called Ione Are, by name of hir father (a sorie sheepheard) Iames of Are, and Isabell hir mother; brought vp poorelie in their trade of keeping cattell . . . Of fauour was she counted likesome, of person stronglie made and manlie, of courage great, hardie, and stout withall: an vnderstander of counsels though she were not at them; great semblance of chastitie both of bodie and behauiour. . . . A person (as their bookes make hir) raised vp by power diuine, onelie for succour to the French estate then deepelie in distresse. . . . From saint Katharins church of Fierbois in Touraine (where she neuer had beene and knew not) in a secret place there among old iron, appointed she hir sword to be sought out and brought hir, that with fiue floure delices was grauen on both sides, wherewith she fought and did

manie slaughters by hir owne hands. . . . Vnto the
Dolphin into his gallerie when first she was brought,
and he shadowing himselfe behind, setting other gaie
lords before him to trie hir cunning, from all the com-
panie, with a salutation . . . she pickt him out alone;
who therevpon had hir to the end of the gallerie,
where she held him an houre in secret and priuate
talke, that of his priuie chamber was thought verie
long, and therefore would haue broken it off; but he
made them a sign to let hir saie on. In which (among
other), as likelie it was, she set out vnto him the
singular feats (forsooth) giuen her to vnderstand by
reuelation diuine, that in vertue of that sword shee
should atchiue; which were, how with honor and vic-
torie shee would raise the siege at Orleance, set him
in state of the crowne of France, and driue the English out of the countrie, thereby he to inioie the king-
dome alone. Heerevpon he hartened at full, appointed hir a sufficient armie with absolute power to
lead them, and they obedientlie to doo as she bad
them.'

The first edition of Holinshed (1577) and the other
earlier English chroniclers are here briefer and quite
different, containing no suggestion of the words out of
which lines 60-68, 98-101, 118 ff. of the play are
developed.[1] Holinshed, however, is by no means the
basis of the entire play. Several scenes—those of
Talbot and the Countess of Auvergne, the rose-
plucking in the Temple Garden, Plantagenet's interview with Mortimer, and Suffolk's capture of Margaret—have no discovered source. The first of these
was probably borrowed from the legend of some popular warrior or outlaw,[2] the others are fanciful embel-
lishments of history.

[1] Holinshed is certainly the source also of IV. i. 18 ff.
See *infra*, p. 144.
[2] The resemblance to Robin Hood stories, suggested by
several critics, is of the vaguest.

In some cases, again, the drama deserts Holinshed in order to make use of the older and generally more detailed chronicle of Edward Halle (*The Union of Lancaster and York,* 1548). This seems to be true of the dialogue between Talbot and his son in IV. v and vi. Holinshed contents himself with a bare summary of the battle at Castillon: 'though he [Talbot] first with manfull courage, and sore fighting wan the entrie of their [the French] campe; yet at length they compassed him about, and shooting him through the thigh with an handgun, slue his horsse, and finally killed him lieng on the ground, whome they durst neuer looke in the face, while he stood on his feet.[1] It was said, that after he perceiued there was no remedie, but present losse of the battell, he counselled his sonne, the lord Lisle, to saue himselfe by flight, sith the same could not redound to anie great reproch in him, this being the first iournie [day of battle] in which he had beene present. Manie words he vsed to persuade him to haue saued his life; but nature so wrought in the son, that neither desire of life, nor feare of death, could either cause him to shrinke, or conueie himselfe out of the danger, and so there manfullie ended his life with his said father.'

Halle, on the other hand, paints the whole scene far more graphically, and suggests some of the actual words which the dramatist puts into Talbot's mouth: 'When the Englishmen were come to the place where the Frenchmen were encamped, in the which (as Æneas Siluius testifieth) were iii. C. peces of brasse, beside diuers other small peces, and subtill Engynes to the Englishmen vnknowen, and nothing suspected, they lyghted al on fote, the erle of Shrewesbury only except, which because of his age, rode on a little hakeney, and fought fiercely with the Frenchmen, &

[1] These words, repeated from Halle, are echoed in I. i. 138-140 of the play.

ʒʊt thentre of their campe, and by fyne force entered
nto the same. This conflicte continued in doubtfull
udgement of victory ii. longe houres: durynge which
ʒight the lordes of Montamban and Humadayre, with
ı great companye of Frenchmen entered the battayle,
ınd began a new felde, & sodaynly the Gonners per-
ʒeiuynge the Englishmen to approche nere, discharged
ʒheir ordinaunce, and slew iii. C. persons, nere to the
ʒrle, who perceiuynge the imminent ieopardy, and
ʒubtile labirynth, in the which he and hys people
were enclosed and illaqueate, despicynge his awne
ʒauegarde, and desirynge the life of his entierly and
welbeloued sonne the lord Lisle, willed, aduertised,
ınd counsailled hym to departe out of the felde, and
ʒo saue hym selfe. But when the sonne had aun-
ʒwered that it was neither honest nor natural for
ʒim, to leue his father in the extreme ieopardye of
ʒis life, and that he woulde taste of that draught,
which his father and Parent should assay and begyn:
ʒhe noble erle & comfortable capitayn sayd to him:
Ɔh sonne sonne, I thy father, which onely hath bene
ʒhe terror and scourge of the French people so many
ʒeres, which hath subuerted so many townes, and
ʒrofligate and discomfited so many of them in open
ʒattayle, and marcial conflict, neither can here dye,
ʒor the honor of my countrey, without great laude
ınd perpetuall fame, nor flye or departe without
ʒerpetuall shame and continualle infamy. But be-
ʒause this is thy first iourney and enterprise, neither
ʒhy flyeng shall redounde to thy shame, nor thy death
ʒo thy glory: for as hardy a man wisely flieth, as a
ʒemerarious person folishely abidethe, therefore ye
ʒeyng of me shalbe ye dishonor, not only of me &
ʒny progenie, but also a discomfiture of all my com-
ʒany: thy departure shall saue thy lyfe, and make
ʒhe able another tyme, if I be slayn to reuenge my
ʒeath and to do honor to thy Prince and profyt to his
Realme. But nature so wrought in the sonne, that

neither desire of lyfe, nor thought of securitie, could
withdraw or pluck him from his natural father: Who
consideryng the constancy of his chyld, and the great
daunger that they stode in, comforted his souldiours,
cheared his Capitayns, and valeauntly set on his
enemies, and slew of them more in number than he
had in his company.   But his enemies hauyng a
greater company of men, & more abundaunce of
ordinaunce then before had bene sene in a battayle,
fyrst shot him through the thyghe with a handgonne,
and slew his horse, & cowardly killed him, lyenge on
the ground, whome they neuer durste loke in the face,
whyle he stode on his fete, and with him, there dyed
manfully hys sonne the lord Lisle. . . .'

Verbal echoes of the passage above are probably
to be found in lines 18, 40, 45, 46 of IV. v and in
line 30 of the next scene.[1]

---

[1] It is fair to observe that the verbal indebtedness to
Halle is not as close as the indebtedness to Holinshed in the
extract given on p. 128, and is very likely a debt at second
hand.   That is, Halle's dialogue between father and son
may have been utilized by the original author of the play,
and Shakespeare, rewriting the scene without direct reference to Halle, may have removed much of Halle's wording,
though leaving enough to show that Shakespeare's authority,
Holinshed, did not furnish all the material.   Moreover, it
is impossible to say whether the original dramatist used
Halle's Chronicle itself or resorted to the later work of
Grafton (1569), for Grafton incorporates the entire passage verbatim.   The only change he makes is to remove
three words of Halle, which he evidently regarded as
archaic.   Instead of 'illaqueate' he reads 'wrapped'; instead of 'profligate and discomfited,' 'discomfited' alone;
and instead of 'temerarious,' 'rashe.'

APPENDIX B

THE HISTORY OF THE PLAY

The drama now known as *1 Henry VI* is first heard of as 'Harry the Sixth' on March 3, 1592. Upon that afternoon it was acted at the Rose Theatre by Lord Strange's Men (Shakespeare's company), who had begun their temporary occupancy of the Rose about a fortnight before (February 19). Philip Henslowe's diary notes that the play was new on March 3, and that the first performance brought the manager the unusually large sum of £3 16s. 8d. It was then repeated with gradually diminishing frequency and returns: the diary records fourteen (possibly fifteen) productions up to June 19, 1592. *Harry the Sixth* appears to have been, as Fleay calls it, the most popular play of its season. Clear evidence of its effect upon the audiences at this time is given in Thomas Nashe's *Pierce Penniless,* written in the summer of 1592 and licensed for the press on August 8. Nashe uses the play to illustrate his argument that the drama may exert a valuable moral influence. 'How would it haue ioyed braue *Talbot* (the terror of the French),' he writes, 'to thinke that after he had lyne two hundred yeares in his Tombe. he should triumphe againe on the Stage, and haue his bones newe embalmed with the teares of ten thousand spectators at least (at seuerall times), who, in the Tragedian that represents his person, imagine they behold him fresh bleeding.' (McKerrow's ed. I. 212.)

There is no reason for doubting that the play referred to in both the documents of 1592 just cited is *1 Henry VI.* There seems nothing, however, to justify the usual assumption that this play had already received Shakespeare's additions, and was therefore in 1592 a revised version of a still earlier drama. Henslowe directly and Nashe by implication testify that their play was new. The same conclusion is warranted by the evident sensation it created in 1592 and particularly by the absence of the smallest hint of its existence previously. The only fair inference, then, from the facts known is that the play of *Harry the Sixth,* dealing largely with Talbot's wars in France, was composed about the beginning of the year 1592, and that this was later remodelled by Shakespeare into *1 Henry VI.*

It is not easy to say when the remodelling and the consequent revival of the play on the stage occurred. In the absence of positive records, critics have naturally inclined to the assumption that a work clearly not equal to Shakespeare's ordinary performances must have been produced very early in his career. Against this are to be weighed the following considerations: (1) The success of Henslowe's play was proved but not completely exploited in 1592. According to the usual methods of the time a revised version would not be called for till after the lapse of several years. Marlowe's *Doctor Faustus,* originally produced about 1589, still held the stage in no seriously altered form from September, 1594, till October, 1597. The first extensive adaptation recorded was paid for, November 22, 1602. *The Jew of Malta,* acted without change from February, 1592, till June, 1596, was revived in 1601. The old *Hamlet,* performed between 1589 and 1594, was rewritten by Shakespeare about 1601.

(2) *1 Henry VI,* as we have it, is arranged to serve as a prologue to *2* and *3 Henry VI.* Shakespeare clearly revised our play with these dramas in his mind, and probably not till after he had completed his revision of them.

(3) The earlier (pre-Shakespearean) versions of *2* and *3 Henry VI* were printed in 1594 and 1595 respectively, these texts presumably becoming accessible to the publishers after the revised dramas supplanted them for stage purposes. The fact that no such text of the early *1 Henry VI* was printed would suggest that that play was reserved either till it was too late to warrant publishers to trade upon its former popularity or till Shakespeare's company began to take more stringent measures to prevent the publication of any play-texts.

(4) A mutual connection exists between *1 Henry VI* and *Henry V* (cf. note on IV. ii. 10, 11). Several passages in our play seem reminiscent of the other (written in 1599). It is a plausible hypothesis at least that *1 Henry VI* was revised in order on the one hand to profit by the popular interest in *Henry V* and on the other to link that play with *2 Henry VI,* thus completing the chain of history dramas from *Richard II* to *Richard III*.[1]

[1] It is often argued that the priority of *1 Henry VI* to *Henry V* is proved by the closing lines of the epilogue to the latter play:

'Henry the Sixth, in infant bands crown'd King
Of France and England, did this king succeed;
Whose state so many had the managing,
That they lost France and made his England bleed:
Which oft our stage hath shown; and, for their sake,
In your fair minds let this acceptance take.'

Dogmatism on the point is not justifiable, but the performance of *Harry the Sixth* in 1592 (and afterward) by Shakespeare's company explains the allusion quite as well as the assumption that the revised *1 Henry VI* had already been acted. I find it easier to read in the lines of the epilogue a modestly veiled hint that if *Henry V* proved a success, Shakespeare was thinking of following it up by a revised version of *Harry the Sixth,* than to believe that he really meant to imply that the *Henry VI* plays as now known were such excellent works as to make amends for any defects in *Henry V*. The epilogue to *2 Henry IV* promised

(5) The most positive evidence of the date of the Shakespearean additions to *1 Henry VI* is that discussed in the note on IV. vii. 63-71. Unless some earlier printed source than is now known can be found for Talbot's epitaph, it will be hard to establish a date prior to 1599 for the revised play.

The idea that Shakespeare could not about 1600 have done work as apparently immature as that which he contributed to *1 Henry VI*, or have sanctioned the performance at that time of so poor a play, is not in consonance with facts. Shakespeare's company undoubtedly produced worse plays during this period when the public taste seemed to warrant them (e.g., *A Yorkshire Tragedy* in 1605), and the Shakespearean parts of *1 Henry VI* are assuredly not as unworthy of the author of *Henry V* as is *The Merry Wives of Windsor* (ca. 1600) unworthy of the author of *Twelfth Night* and *Much Ado About Nothing*.

On November 8, 1623, the publishers of the Shakespeare Folio, Blount and Jaggard, entered our play for publication under the rather surprising title of 'The thirde parte of Henry ye Sixt.' The work now known as *1 Henry VI* is certainly meant, for *2* and *3 Henry VI* (in their early forms) had both been previously licensed,[1] and the Blount-Jaggard license specifically refers only to such of Shakespeare's plays 'as are not formerly entred to other men.' It is probable that in thus listing as the third part the drama which by historical sequence became in the Folio the first part, the publishers meant more

the audience *Henry V*, 'if you be not too much cloyed.' The epilogue to *Henry V* reminds them how they have in the past applauded *Henry VI*. Is it not the intention to suggest: 'Perhaps you may have those plays again' (with *Harry the Sixth* worked over so as to fill its place in the series)?

[1] When Millington assigned the early versions of *2* and *3 Henry VI* to Pavier, April 19, 1602, he called them 'the first and second parte of Henry the VI.'

than simply that this was the last part remaining un-
licensed. It seems fair to assume that they so thought
of it because they remembered it as the latest of
Shakespeare's *Henry VI* plays to be produced on the
stage.

Since Shakespeare's death, *1 Henry VI* has had
only the scantiest stage history. Most subsequent
adaptations of the Henry VI cycle ignore the first
part. However, J. H. Merivale's compilation, *Richard, Duke of York,* acted by Edmund Kean, December
22, 1817, and published the same year, opens with
three scenes closely following II. iv, II. v, III. i,
and IV. i of our play.

An abridgment of the three *Henry VI* plays
('*Henry VI.* A Tragedy in Five Acts. Condensed
from Shakespeare, and arranged for the Stage') was
prepared by the eminent actor-manager, Charles
Kemble (1775-1854), and first printed from the only
known copy in volume ii of the *Henry Irving Shakespeare.* This work begins like Merivale's with the
Temple Garden scene, and like it ignores the scenes
in France. *1 Henry VI* furnished Kemble with the
material for Act I (approximately) of his adaptation,
which seems never to have been acted.

On March 13, 1738, 'by desire of several Ladies
of Quality' the play of 'Henry 6th, part 1st,' was
performed for the benefit of the actor Dennis Delane
(died, 1750), who acted Talbot to the Suffolk of
Walker and the Joan of Arc of Mrs. Hallam. The
notice 'not acted fifty years,' affixed to the announce-
ment of this performance, appears to be a most con-
servative under-statement. The most remarkable
recent production was that given by the F. R. Benson
company at the Stratford Memorial Festival in May,
1906. Mr. Benson here 'made a triumphant Talbot,
and the audience seemed never weary of recalling
him.' (*Athenæum,* May 12, 1906.)

APPENDIX C

THE AUTHORSHIP OF THE PLAY

I. SHAKESPEARE'S CONCERN IN IT

With regard to the connection of Shakespeare with
1 Henry VI four different opinions have been put
forward:

(1) Shakespeare had no part in the play.   This
was apparently the view of Richard Farmer, who
says (*Essay on the Learning of Shakespeare*, 1767):
'*Henry the sixth* hath ever been doubted; and
[Nashe's allusion in *Pierce Penniless*] may give us
reason to believe it was previous to our Author. . . .
I have no doubt but *Henry the sixth* had the same
Author with *Edward the third.*' Malone[1] and Drake[2]
took the negative position strongly, and Collier flirted
with it,[3] while more recently Dowden (*Shakspere:
His Mind and Art*, 173; *Shakspere Primer*, etc.) and
Furnivall (Introduction to *Leopold Shakspere*) have
virtually denied any real trace of Shakespeare in the
work.

(2) Shakespeare wrote the entire play.   Samuel
Johnson favored this hypothesis, arguing that 'from
mere inferiority nothing can be inferred; in the productions of wit there will be inequality.'   He was
supported by his colleague Steevens, who remarks:

[1] Boswell-Malone Shakespeare, 1823, v. 246: 'I am therefore decisively of opinion that this play was not written
by Shakspeare'; ibid., xviii. 557: Part I is 'the entire or
nearly the entire production of some ancient dramatist.'
[2] *Shakspeare and his Times*, 1817, ii. 293: 'The hand of
Shakspeare is nowhere visible throughout the entire of this
"Drum-and-Trumpet-Thing," as Mr. Morgan [Maurice Mor-
gann] has justly termed it.'
[3] *Annals of the Stage*, 1831, iii. 145: 'It is plausibly con-
jectured that Shakespeare never touched the *First Part of
Henry VI* as it stands in his works.'

''This historical play might have been one of our author's earliest dramatick efforts; and almost every young poet begins his career by imitation. Shakspeare therefore, till he felt his own strength, perhaps servilely conformed to the style and manner of his predecessors.'[1] Charles Knight in the *Pictorial Shakspeare* (1867) asserted with much greater positiveness that all the three parts of *Henry VI* 'are, in the strictest sense of the word, Shakspeare's own plays,' and was followed by the American critics, Verplanck (1847) and Hudson.[2] Such has been the view almost unanimously of the Germans: Schlegel, Bodenstedt, Delius, Ulrici, Sarrazin, Brandl, Creizenach (Gervinus is the honorable exception). The only recent British scholar to espouse this cause is, I believe, Courthope,[3] who in a remarkable Appendix 'On the Authenticity of Some of the Early Plays Assigned to Shakespeare and their Relationship to the Development of his Dramatic Genius' (*History*

[1] Capell also should apparently be included among the believers in Shakespeare's exclusive authorship. In his introduction he anticipates and very quaintly develops the idea of Steevens's second sentence: 'We are quite in the dark as to when the first part was written; but should be apt to conjecture, that it was some considerable time after the other two; and perhaps when those two were retouched. . . . And those two parts, even with all their retouchings, being still much inferior to the other plays of that class, he may reasonably [*sic*] be supposed to have underwrit himself on purpose in the first, that it might the better match with those it belong'd to.'

[2] 'I can but give it as my firm and settled judgment that the main body of the play is certainly Shakespeare's; nor do I perceive any clear and decisive reason for calling in another hand to account for any part of it.'

[3] Note, however, the historian Gairdner's passing remark (*Studies in English History,* 1881, 65): 'I dismiss altogether the hypothesis which some have advanced, that the First Part of *Henry VI* was not really Shakespeare's. So far as internal evidence goes, if in ability it be not equal to Shakespeare's best, it is too great for any other writer.'

of English Poetry, vol. iv, 1903) goes even farther
than Knight.

(3) Shakespeare collaborated with other drama-
tists to produce the play.   Grant White (*Essay on
the Authorship of King Henry the Sixth,* 1859) sup-
poses that 'It is not improbable that Marlowe, Greene,
Peele, and Shakespeare were all engaged upon it,'
and suggests 'that within two or three years of Shakespeare's arrival in London, that is, about 1587 or
1588, he was engaged to assist Marlowe, Greene, and
perhaps Peele, in dramatizing the events of King
Henry the Sixth's reign.'   Ingram (*Marlowe and his
Associates,* 1904) writes that *1 Henry VI* 'furnishes
but slight evidence of containing much of the handi-
work of the two men, Marlowe and Shakespeare, who
are now believed [*sic*] to have jointly remodelled it';
and Hart (*Arden Shakespeare,* 1909) reasons: 'We
are at liberty to place Part I, in so far as it is Shakespeare's, as his earliest work with a date of about
1589-90. . . . I see no reason, therefore, to look for
an imaginary earlier completed play. . . . We can
imagine very easily that Shakespeare was invited to
lend a hand to Greene and Peele.'

(4) Shakespeare, working by himself, revised an
earlier play of different authorship.   Theobald seems
first to have formulated this theory: 'Though there
are several master-strokes in these three plays [of
Henry VI], which incontestably betray the workman-
ship of Shakspeare; yet I am almost doubtful
whether they were entirely of his writing.   And unless they were wrote by him very early, I should
rather imagine them to have been brought to him as
a director of the stage; and so have received some
finishing beauties at his hand.'[1]   Such is the opinion
of Coleridge, Gervinus, Staunton, Halliwell-Phillipps,

[1] This is the sense also of Maurice Morgann's wild obiter
dictum on the play, referred to in the quotation from Drake
above.   He alludes to Sir John Fastolfe. 'a name for ever

and Dyce, the last of whom definitely repudiates the Grant White theory: 'not written by Shakespeare in conjunction with any other author or authors, but . . . a comparatively old drama, which he slightly altered and improved.' Fleay gives precise, but highly dubious, details (*Life and Work of Shakspere*, 1886): 'About 1588-9 Marlowe plotted, and, in conjunction with Kyd (or Greene), Peele, and Lodge, wrote *1 Henry VI* for the Queen's men. . . . In 1591-2 the Queen's men were in distress and sold, among other plays, *1 Henry VI* to Lord Strange's men, who produced it in 1592 with Shakspere's Talbot additions as a new play.' Rives (1874) argues that Shakespeare revised and expanded an old play dealing exclusively with the wars in France, and Henneman (1901) comes to much the same conclusion. Gray (1917) allows Shakespeare's revisionary labor a somewhat less wide, but still very extensive scope. Herford (Eversley Shakespeare), Rolfe, and Sir Sidney Lee limit the signs of his hand to a couple of scenes; while Ward, Gollancz and Schelling stress their belief that Shakespeare was not properly a reviser, but a 'contributor' of 'additions' to the original work.

This last theory, with its differing implications, has vastly the largest number of upholders at the present time, and is indeed the only one that can be brought into reasonable harmony with the evidence. In regard to the particular scenes to be ascribed to Shakespeare there has been no radical variation among good critics. Nearly all credit Shakespeare

dishonoured by a frequent exposure in that Drum-and-trumpet Thing called *The first part of Henry VI.*, written doubtless, or rather exhibited, long before *Shakespeare* was born, tho' afterwards repaired, I think, and furbished up by him with here and there a little sentiment and diction.' (*Essay on the Dramatic Character of Sir John Falstaff*, 1777.)

with II. iv (the Temple Garden dispute); a large majority also with II. v (the death of Mortimer), which naturally links itself with the foregoing, and with the whole or most of IV. ii-vii (Talbot's death). With less assurance V. iii. 45-195 (Suffolk's wooing of Margaret) is added. In all these there are strong indications of Shakespeare. Note the plays on words: 'I love no colours, and without all colour' (II. iv. 34); 'And in that ease, I'll tell thee my disease' (II. v. 44); 'And they shall find dear deer of us' (IV. ii. 54), together with the technical deer-hunting allusions in the last passage and the hawk, dog, horse references in II. iv. 11-14.

Compare also the bold use of transferred adjectives, quite Shakespearean and quite unlike the general style of the play as a whole: 'In dumb significants' (II. iv. 26), 'this pale and maiden blossom' (II. iv. 47), 'this pale and angry rose' (II. iv. 107), 'my blood-drinking hate' (II. iv. 108), 'death and deadly night' (II. iv. 127), 'feet whose strengthless stay is numb' (II. v. 13), 'sweet enlargement' (II. v. 30), 'the dusky torch of Mortimer' (II. v. 122), 'your stately and air-braving towers' (IV. ii. 13), 'the process of his sandy hour' (IV. ii. 36), 'sleeping neglection' (IV. iii. 49), 'That ever living man of memory' (IV. iii. 51), 'bring thy father to his drooping chair' (IV. v. 5), 'bold-fac'd victory' (IV. vi. 12).

Especially Shakespearean are the fanciful metaphors and similes which abound in these scenes: 'Were growing time once ripen'd to my will' (II. iv. 99); 'I'll note you in my book of memory' (II. iv. 101); 'these gray locks, the pursuivants of Death' (II. v. 5); 'These eyes, like lamps whose wasting oil is spent' (II. v. 8); 'pithless arms, like to a wither'd vine That droops his sapless branches to the ground' (II. v. 11, 12); 'Just death, kind umpire of men's miseries' (II. v. 29); 'But now thy uncle is removing hence, As princes do their courts, when they are cloy'd With long continuance in a settled place' (II. v. 104-106); 'To wall thee from the liberty of flight' (IV. ii. 24); 'girdled with a waist of iron' (IV. iii. 20); 'ring'd about with bold adversity' (IV. iv. 14); 'Now thou art seal'd the son of chivalry' (IV. vi. 29); 'To save a paltry life and slay bright fame' (IV. vi. 45); 'Triumphant death, smear'd with captivity' (IV. vii. 3); 'inhearsed in the arms Of the most bloody nurser of his harms' (IV. vii. 46); 'Twinkling another counterfeited beam' (V. iii. 63).

Consideration of the passages just cited, which are fairly representative, though of course not complete, will, I think, suggest a gradual decrease through the scenes concerned in the recognizable Shakespearean quality. The Temple Garden and Mortimer scenes are rather more positively like Shakespeare than the blank verse Talbot passages, and decidedly more so than the rimed Talbot passages (IV. iii. 28-46, IV. v. 16-vii. 50) or the Suffolk-Margaret scene. This is reasonable, since the first two scenes bear most appearance of being spontaneous with the reviser of the play, and since Shakespeare's language is regularly bolder in blank verse than in rime.

It would be hazardous to attempt to infer from the style alone the date at which Shakespeare wrote his scenes.[1] The diction does not seem to me that of the poet's earliest period; and Furnivall has observed that the proportion of extra-syllabled lines in the Temple Garden scene (about 26 per cent) 'forbids us supposing it is very early work.' It would also be ill-advised to set precise limits for Shakespeare's part in the play. His hand is most evident in the scenes just discussed, but Talbot's death must, I think, have been a conspicuous feature of the original pre-Shakespearean play, and it is unlikely that the reviser here removed all traces of his predecessor. On

[1] See the Appendix on The History of the Play, p. 134.

the other hand, it is entirely reasonable to suspect
Shakespearean penciling in scenes where the hand-
ling is too light or too perfunctory to leave any defi-
nite impression of genius.   In particular, Mr. Gray
finds evidence of the greater writer in the opening
of III. i and in the Vernon-Basset quarrel (III. iv.
28 ff. and IV. i. 78 ff.).   I am impressed by Henneman's suggestion that IV. i as a whole is the reviser's
replica of III. iv (cf. note on IV. i): there seems to
be nothing in the later scene which Shakespeare
might not have written, and a positive clue may perhaps be found in the fact that Talbot's account of
the Battle of Patay is here certainly taken from
Holinshed rather than Halle.[1]   Another hint of the
same kind appears in I. ii in the adoption from Holinshed's second edition of the favorable view of Joan
of Arc (which Holinshed explains that he derives
from French sources), whereas the remainder of the
play gives an inharmonious conception drawn from
the earlier English chronicles.[2]

The reviser's hand, presumably Shakespeare's, is
evident in the way the close of *1 Henry VI* is shaped
to fit it as an introduction to Part II of the trilogy.
Henneman states the relationship of the three parts
with accuracy, if with undue caution: 'So specifically
does I prepare for II and III in certain particulars
that it is conceivable that I was written after II and
that III had already been planned.'   If he means in

[1] Holinshed reports that Talbot had 'not past six thousand men' (cf. IV. i. 20 and also I. i. 112), while Halle gives
him five thousand.
[2] Two small points, which I have not seen mentioned,
may have some bearing on the date of Shakespeare's revision: (1) The Mortimer scene, especially lines 67-81,
sounds rather like a reminiscence of *1 Henry IV*.
(2) Margaret's vain efforts to make Suffolk attend to her
questions and the retribution she takes (V. iii. 72-109) repeat Falstaff's tactics with the Chief Justice (*2 Henry IV*,
II. i. 184-211).   It is possible, but hardly so likely, that the
sequence was the other way.

the case of Part I, not the original composition, but the reviser's adaptation, it is certain, I think, that I follows II. Note that the thirty-ninth line of the play, where Winchester says to Gloucester, 'Thy wife is proud; she holdeth thee in awe,' can only be rationally explained as a preparation for Part II. The gibe means nothing as regards Part I. Again, the conclusion of Part I can only have been worked into an open advertisement for Part II,

'Margaret shall now be queen, and rule the king;
But I will rule both her, the king, and realm,'

after Parts II and III had passed into the possession of Shakespeare's company, and been adapted for representation by them. The 1592 *Harry the Sixth* cannot well be imagined to have ended so, for Pembroke's company appear at this time to have owned the early versions of Parts II and III.[1] It is not reasonable that Strange's company should have employed a conclusion quite out of keeping with their main theme of Talbot's glory and explicable only as preparing the audience for the play of a rival company.

That the original ending of the play was greatly changed by the reviser appears from textual evidence, which Fleay with characteristic subtlety noted, and, I think, characteristically misinterpreted. The marking of acts and scenes in the only early edition—that of the Folio—is entirely regular as far as the close of Act III (save that the individual scenes of Acts I and II are not divided off); and it is extraordinarily chaotic in Acts IV and V. Practically the whole close of the play (from IV. i through V. iv) is given

[1] Pembroke's Men are supposed to have sold these plays and others at the time of their distress in September, 1593— a year and a half after Strange's (Shakespeare's) Men produced *Harry the Sixth*. Cf. Greg, *Henslowe's Diary*, ii. 85; Murray, *English Dram. Companies*, i. 65. (I do not agree with Murray's suggestion of a possible connection between Shakespeare and the Pembroke company.)

as Act IV, Act V consisting only of the short last
scene (V. v), and being marked at all probably
merely in order to secure the conventional total of
five acts. The six scenes dealing with Talbot's death
(IV. ii-vii) are undivided and carelessly tacked on
to IV. i, with which they have only a remote organic
connection. From this Fleay argues that the Talbot
scenes are a patch of new material, not corresponding
to anything in the old play: 'It is plain that they
were written subsequently to the rest of the play and
inserted at a revival. They had to be inserted in
such a manner as not to break the connection between
this play and *2 Henry VI;* and were put in the most
convenient place, regardless of historic sequence.' I
think the reverse is true: that it was the necessity of
creating a spurious connection with *2 Henry VI* which
produced the disorder. Originally the Talbot scenes
probably came nearer the end of the play and stood
in closer relationship to their natural complement,
the retributive overthrow of Joan (V. ii, iii. 1-44, iv.
1-93) and the final submission of the Dauphin (V. iv.
116-175). On this unhistorical, but very dramatic
note of national vindication the old play may be supposed to have concluded. To change this note to that
of pessimism and foreboding with which Part II
opens was the reviser's problem.[1] It required a complete *volte-face,* which has been executed with dex-
terity but probably at a cost to the effectiveness of
this play (considered individually and not as the
introduction to a great tetralogy) for which Shakespeare's improvement of the poetry in the Talbot
scenes does not compensate. The patchwork is most
painfully evident where the otherwise admirable
Suffolk-Margaret-Reignier scene (V. iii. 45-195) is
pasted in between two sections of the Joan story.

[1] The clearest indication of an effort to prepare the
audience for this new gloom in the close appears in the
croaking speeches of Exeter, affixed to III. i and IV. i.

The last scene in the play, constituting the entire
Actus Quintus of the Folio, clearly belongs altogether
to the later recension. The writing of so purely
utilitarian a scene was small game for Shakespeare,
but the execution is by no means un-Shakespearean.[1]

Henneman's summary of Shakespeare's probable
purpose in *1 Henry VI* is, I think, fair and conserva-
tive: 'To work up or rewrite the Talbot portions of
the Chronicles, probably, though not necessarily,
already crystallized into an old play on the triumph
of "brave Talbot" over the French, which possessed
the hated Joan of Arc scenes and all; to intensify the
figure and character of Talbot; to work over or add
scenes like those touching Talbot's death; to connect
him with the deplorable struggles of the nobles; to
invent, by a happy poetical thought, the origin of the
factions of the Red and White Roses in the Temple
Garden; to sound at once the note of weakness in the
king continued in the succeeding Parts, and thus con-
vert the old Talbot material effectually into a Henry
VI drama; and to close with the wooing of Margaret
as specific introduction to Part II,—something like
this seems the task that the dramatist set himself to
perform.'

II. The Author of the Original Play

1. *Marlowe ?*

Henslowe's play of *Harry the Sixth*, if it followed
somewhat the lines just suggested, undoubtedly de-
served the popularity it attained. It was probably
more effective on the stage than the expanded work
which supplanted it, and in 1591-92 can have been

---

[1] Gervinus pointed out (*Shakespeare*, 2d ed., 1850, i. 202)
that if the Suffolk-Margaret scene and the last scene were
omitted, and the play left to close with 'Winchester's peace'
(V. iv), it would have a conclusion much better suited to
the chief content.

written only by a real poet and a skilled dramatist.
There were not many such at this period. Marlowe
was one, but I concur warmly in Mr. Gray's opinion
that 'Marlowe himself cannot be read into this
drama.' Marlowe's influence, however, is unquestion-
ably apparent in the older parts of the play. Note,
for example, the following echoes:[1]

I. i. 2:
   'Comets, importing change of times and states'
Marlowe's Lucan 527:
   'And comets that presage the fall of kingdoms.'

I. i. 3:
   'Brandish your crystal tresses in the sky.'
Tamburlaine 1922:
   'Shaking her silver tresses in the air.'

I. i. 22:
   'Like captives bound to a triumphant car.'
Edward II 174:
   'With captive kings at his triumphant car.'

I. i. 36:
   'Whom like a school-boy you may over-awe.'
Edward II 1336 f.:
   'As though your highness were a school-boy still,
   And must be awed and governed like a child.'

I. i. 46:
   'Instead of gold we'll offer up our arms.'
Jew of Malta 758 f.:
                   'Instead of gold,
   We'll send thee bullets wrapped in smoke and fire.'

I. i. 149:
   'I'll hale the Dauphin headlong from his throne.'
Tamburlaine 4021:
   'Haling him headlong to the lowest hell.'

I. vi. 11, 12:
   'Why ring not out the bells throughout the town?
   Dauphin, command the citizens make bonfires.'
Tamburlaine 1335 f.:
   'Ringing with joy their superstitious bells,
   And making bonfires for my overthrow.'

   [1] The line numbers for Marlowe's works are those of the
Oxford edition.

III. ii. 40:
'That hardly we escap'd the pride of France.'
Tamburlaine 140:
'Lest you subdue the pride of Christendom.'
Tamburlaine 3568:
'To overdare the pride of Græcia.'
Dido 482:
'That after burnt the pride of Asia.'

III. ii. 136:
'But kings and mightiest potentates must die.'
Tamburlaine 4641:
'For Tamburlaine, the scourge of God, must die.'

III. iii. 13:
'And we will make thee famous through the world.'
Tamburlaine 2173:
'And makes my deeds infamous through the world.'

III. iii. 24:
'But be extirped from our provinces.'
Faustus 122:
'And reign sole king of all our provinces.'

IV. vii. 32:
'Now my old arms are young John Talbot's grave.'
Jew of Malta 1192:
'These arms of mine shall be thy sepulchre.'

V. iv. 34:
'Take her away; for she hath liv'd too long.'
Edward II 2651:
'Nay, to my death, for too long have I lived.'

V. iv. 87, 88:
'May never glorious sun reflex his beams
Upon the country where you make abode.'
Tamburlaine 969 f.:
'For neither rain can fall upon the earth,
Nor sun reflex his virtuous beams thereon.'

Marlowe's general influence is also traceable, as in
I. vi, where the barbaric magnificence of the Dauphin's
promises to Joan plagiarizes those of Tamburlaine to
Zenocrate (*Tamb.* 278 ff.), and his promise that Joan's
coffin shall be carried before the kings and queens of
France recalls the second part of Marlowe's play
(II. iii, III. ii). The concluding couplet of this same

scene echoes the close of *1 Tamburlaine,* Act III; and
the burial of Zenocrate is again clearly parodied in
the burial of Salisbury (II. ii).[1]

All this means mimicry, conscious or unconscious.
Frequently the imitation degenerates into travesty,
as in the weak mouthing of Bedford (I. i. 148-156)
and the atrocious rot of the whole scene in which
Salisbury is stricken (I. iv). Imagine Marlowe
making his chief hero say at the height of passion:

'What chance is this, that suddenly hath cross'd us?
Speak, Salisbury; at least, if thou canst speak,' etc.

It is easier to conceive the mighty line to have attained the unsurpassable flatness of the messenger's
words in II. iii. 29, 30:

'Stay, my Lord Talbot; for my Lady craves
To know the cause of your abrupt departure.'

The real proof that Marlowe did not write *Harry
the Sixth* is the absence of any passion except in
scenes which bear marks of revision. The lines are
usually musical and sometimes charming, and the
stage action is interesting, but they are not irradiated
by the electric intensity that scintillates in Marlowe.
Till Shakespeare vivifies him in the fourth act, Talbot
himself is but a skeleton in armor.

2.   *Greene ?*

Greene has been very often suggested as the author
of this play, most recently by Gray, though with
reservations, and most positively by Hart. I see
nothing that renders such an attribution reasonable:
Hart's verbal parallels seem quite without demon-
strative value. Greene's essays in the chronicle his-

---

[1] Several of these similarities have been noted by Anders,
Shakespeare's Books, p. 121. Sarrazin had previously mentioned the resemblance of Joan's appeal to Burgundy (III.
iii) and Tamburlaine's appeal to Theridamas (305 ff.).

tory drama are notably characteristic, and evidence
a method entirely unlike that of this play. He nowhere exhibits any tendency toward patriotic themes
or any interest in the facts of history. Rather in his
quasi-historic plays, *Friar Bacon and Friar Bungay*
and *James IV* (and in *George-a-Greene* if it be his),
he yields to an apparently irresistible devotion for
pastoral woodland settings, romantic love stories,
quaint supernaturalism, and clownish roguery. Unless one can fancy Joan's brief address to her fiends
(V. iii. 1-24) to be akin in atmosphere or purpose to
the magic humbuggery of Bacon and the fairy ma-
chinery of Oberon, *1 Henry VI* is wholly unlike
Greene in all these points. It is unlike him both in
the inflexibility with which it harps on the historical
note, and in its absence of humor, sentiment, or
pathos. Greene, of course, may have written the
play, but it is less like his avowed work than that
of any contemporary dramatist.

3. *Peele ?*

It is not by a process of elimination merely that I
arrive at George Peele as the most likely author of
the old *Harry the Sixth* play. Indications of several
kinds point in Peele's direction. He was at the time
the work was produced distinctly the most conspicuous exponent of jingoistic national pride—a
trait of which Marlowe shows absolutely nothing and
Greene hardly more. Peele had composed the patriotic masques to celebrate the Lord Mayoralty of
Sir Wolstan Dixie in 1585 and of Sir William Web
in 1591. His *Polyhymnia* (1590) lauded in martial
strains 'the honourable Triumph at Tilt' when Sir
Henry Lea formally resigned his post of Queen's
Champion, and he again touched the same theme in
Anglorum Feriae (1595), written in honor of the
thirty-seventh anniversary of Elizabeth's accession.

In 1589 he had twice come forth as the spokesman
of the nation: in his *Eclogue Gratulatory* to the Earl
of Essex 'for his welcome into England from Portu-
gal,' and in his fine *Farewell*, 'Entituled to the famous
and fortunate Generals of our English forces: Sir
John Norris and Sir Francis Drake.' Later, again,
in 1593, he linked the knighthood of his age with
that of the past in *The Honour of the Garter*.[1] His
plays of the same period, *Edward I* and *The Battle
of Alcazar*, are equally filled with the praise of English daring. No known author of 1591 has anything
like the same claim on merely extrinsic evidence to
be regarded as the author of a play in celebration
of the martial exploits of the brave Lord Talbot.[2]

General similarities between Peele's *Edward I* and
1 Henry VI have been often noted, particularly the
unhappy resemblance in the defamation of the Span-
ish Eleanor and the French Joan of Arc. One of
the most insular of Britons, Peele was incapable of
glorifying his countrymen without slandering the
races they opposed. The undramatic line put into
Joan's mouth (III. iii. 85),

'Done like a Frenchman: turn, and turn again!'

is fairly characteristic of his bigotry.

The verse of the older portions of the play—
saccharine rather than strong, and the loose but
animated structure are what one finds in Peele's
recognized dramas. The imitation of Marlowe is

---

[1] This poem should be compared with Talbot's speech,
'When first this order was ordained,' etc. (IV. i. 33 ff.).

[2] Peele's favorite epigram, which he affixes at least
three times to his poems, might well serve as motto for
1 Henry VI:

'Gallia victa dedit flores, invicta leones
    Anglia, jus belli in flore, leone suum;
O sic, O semper ferat Anglia laeta (or 'Elizabetha')
    triumphos,
Inclyta Gallorum flore, leone suo.'

equally a feature of those which were produced after *Tamburlaine.*[1]

The Countess of Auvergne episode, with its grace and lack of human warmth, seems to me like Peele's work. In its relation to the military plot, and particularly in the military tableau with which it closes, it is very suggestive of the more elaborated Countess

---

[1] *Edward I* 954:
  'It is but temporal that you can inflict.'
  Edward II 1550:
  'Tis but temporal that thou canst inflict.'

  Edward I 1165 f.:
  'This comfort, madam, that your grace doth give
  Binds me in double duty whilst I live.'
  Edward II 1684 f.:
  'These comforts that you give our woeful queen
  Bind us in kindness all at your command.'

  Edward I 2800:
  'Hence, feigned weeds, unfeigned is my grief.'
  Edward II 1964:
  'Hence, feigned weeds, unfeigned are my woes.'

  David & Bethsabe 12-14:
  'The host of heaven . . . cast
  Their crystal armor at his conquering feet.'
  Tamburlaine 1932:
  'There angels in their crystal armors fight.'

  David & Bethsabe 181:
  'And makes their weapons wound the senseless winds.'
  Tamburlaine 1256:
  'And make our strokes to wound the senseless air'
      ('lure' in first edition).

  Battle of Alcazar 190:
  'The bells of Pluto ring revenge amain.'
  Edward II 1956:
  'Let Pluto's bells ring out my fatal knell.'

  Battle of Alcazar 250:
  'Tamburlaine, triumph not, for thou must die.'
  Tamburlaine 4641:
  'For Tamburlaine, the Scourge of God, must die.'

(The line numbers for Peele's plays are those of the Malone Society editions.)

of Salisbury episode in the anonymous *Edward III.*
I give my adhesion to the conjecture of Farmer, already quoted, that '*Henry the sixth* [in its earliest
form] had the same Author with *Edward the third,*'
and believe that author to have been Peele.[1]

APPENDIX D

THE TEXT OF THE PRESENT EDITION

The text of the present volume is, by permission
of the Oxford University Press, that of the Oxford
Shakespeare, edited by the late W. J. Craig, except
for the following deviations:

1.   The stage directions are those of the original
Folio edition, necessary additional words being inserted in square brackets.

2.   The punctuation has been altered in many
places, and the spelling normalized in the following
instances: French place names in general (e.g.,
Champagne, Gisors, Poitiers, Bordeaux instead of
Champaigne, Guysors, Poictiers, Bourdeaux); antic
(antick), everywhere (every where), forfend (fore-
fend), forgo (forego), immortaliz'd (immortalis'd),
warlike (war-like).

3.   The following alterations of the text have been
made after collation with the Folio, readings of the
present edition preceding and those of Craig following the colon.   Except in the one case otherwise
marked the changes all represent a return to the
Folio text:

    I. ii. 41   gimmors: gimmals
    I. iv. 28   Call'd: Called
        95   thee: thee, Nero
    I. v. 16   hungry-starved: hunger-starved

[1] Cf. *The Shakespeare Apocrypha,* p. xxiii.

I. vi. 22   of: or (F)
II. ii. 54   'tis: it is
II. iv. 6   th' error: the error
II. v. 71   Richard: King Richard
III. i. 25, 114   sovereign: sov'reign
198   lose: should lose
III. ii. 28   Talbonites: Talbotites
III. iii. 76   wandering: wand'ring
IV. i. 138   wavering: wav'ring
IV. ii. 6   sovereign: sov'reign
IV. iii. 28   makes: make
IV. vii. 25   whether: whe'r
65   Verdon: Verdun
V. iii. 68   here: here thy prisoner
153   country: county
V. v. 39   lord: good lord
46   liberal: a liberal

APPENDIX E

SUGGESTIONS FOR COLLATERAL READING

George Lockhart Rives: *An Essay on the First, Second, and Third Parts of Henry the Sixth; Commonly attributed to Shakespeare.* 1874. (Harness Prize Essay. Largely based on Grant White's earlier monograph on the same subject.)

F. G. Fleay: *Who Wrote 'Henry VI'? Macmillan's Magazine*, November, 1875.

Life and Work of Shakspere, 1886, 255-263.

W. H. Egerton: *Talbot's Tomb in the Parish Church of St. Alkmund's, Whitchurch.* In *Transactions of the Shropshire Archæological and Natural History Society*, viii. 413-440, 1885. (An interesting article dealing with the exhumation of Talbot's bones and the evidence derived from them concerning the manner of his death.)

W. G. Boswell-Stone: *Shakspere's Holinshed*, ix. 205-242, 1896.

J. B. Henneman: *The Episodes in Shakespeare's I. Henry VI. In Publications of the Modern Language Association of America,* xv. 290-320, 1900. (An admirable article.)

Sir A. T. Quiller-Couch: *Historical Tales from Shakespeare,* 257-276, 1912.

H. D. Gray: *The Purport of Shakespeare's Contribution to 1 Henry VI. In Publications of the Modern Language Association of America,* xxxii. 367-382, 1917.

The most elaborate edition of the play is that of H. C. Hart (*Arden Shakespeare,* Methuen, 1909. Considerable philological erudition is here vitiated by unsound judgment). Other helpful editions are W. J. Rolfe's (1882); Frank A. Marshall's in vol. i of the *Henry Irving Shakespeare* (1888), containing important introduction and notes; and that in the New Grant White Shakespeare, vol. vi (Little, Brown & Co., 1912).

Students of the play will find it interesting to compare the treatment of Joan of Arc and Talbot with the presentation of the same figures in Voltaire's travesty, *La Pucelle d'Orléans* (first authorized edition, 1762), and in Schiller's ultra-romantic *Jungfrau von Orleans* (1801).

Much important information regarding Sir John Fastolfe and a number of letters written by him will be found in the first volume of Gairdner's edition of the *Paston Letters* (1872). See also Gairdner, *The Historical Element in Shakespeare's Falstaff* in *Studies in English History,* 55-77, 1881; and L. W. Vernon Harcourt, *The Two Sir John Fastolfs* in *Transactions of the Royal Historical Society,* 1910, 47-62. The latter attempts, on interesting but not very convincing evidence, to identify Falstaff with a somewhat older and obscurer namesake of the Fastolfe of *1 Henry VI.*

INDEX OF WORDS GLOSSED

(Figures in full-faced type refer to page-numbers)

www.ingramcontent.com/pod-product-compliance
Lightning Source LLC
Chambersburg PA
CBHW020130180626
46810CB00004B/1494